MASTER YOUR MEMORY

BOOKS, VIDEOS AND AUDIO TAPES
BY TONY BUZAN

Books

Speed Reading
Memory Vision (workbook for *Master Your Memory*)
Use Your Head
Use Your Memory
The Brain User's Guide
Make the Most of Your Mind
Harnessing the ParaBrain
(Business version of *Make the Most of Your Mind*)
Spore One (poetry – Limited Edition)

Video Tapes

Use Your Head
The Enchanted Loom
Buzan Business Training
Family Genius Training

Audio Tapes

Learning and Memory
The Intelligence Revolution
Make the Most of Your Mind
Supercreativity and Mind Mapping

Other Works

The Universal Personal Organiser
'Body and Soul' (Master Mind Map poster)
The Mind Map Kit
Master Your Memory Matrix (SEM^3) *0–10,000*

see Appendix for more information
including how to order these items

MASTER YOUR MEMORY

Tony Buzan

Guild Publishing London

Dedicated to my dear friends in the Brain Clubs and Buzan Centres

With especial thanks to Vanda North for her dedication to and support of the concept, and for playing the memory games with me; to Lorraine Gill, the Artist, for her brilliant research and constant inspiration; to my Personal Assistant Carol Coaker and Research Assistant, Phyllida Wilson; to Christopher Hedley-Dent for his generous help on the information on art, and to my Editor, Tracey May, for a memorable performance!

This edition published 1989
by Guild Publishing
by arrangement with
David & Charles Publishers plc

First published 1988
New and revised edition 1989

Phototypeset by Typesetters (Birmingham) Ltd
Smethwick West Midlands
and printed in Great Britain
by Billings & Sons Ltd Worcester
for David & Charles Publishers plc
Brunel House   Newton Abbot   Devon

CONTENTS

CHAPTER ONE

THE BEGINNING

A student sat enthralled. It was the first lesson of his first day at university. In front of him the Professor was calling the roll:

'Abrahamson?'	'Here, sir!'
'Adams?'	'Here, sir!'
'Barlow?'	'Here, sir!'
'Bush?'	'Here, sir!'
'Buzan?'	'Here, sir!' . . .

There were two things different on this morning from the normal roll call in a class: first, the Professor was standing in front of his own desk, his hands clasped firmly behind his back, with no list of students' names in front of him; second, when he came to the next name, 'Cartland', and there was no response, he did *not* move on to 'Chapman', but paused for a moment his hands still clasped behind his back, his eyes looking straight at the students, and said '*Cartland*!? . . . Jeremy Cartland, address 2761 West Third Avenue; phone number 794 6231; date of birth September 25th 1941; mother's name Jean, father's name Gordon; . . . *Cartland*!? Absent!'

And so the Professor continued, calling the roll without hesitation, and wherever a student was absent, even though he had never seen him before, and could have had no way of knowing, on this first day, who was going to be present and who not, presenting the entire list of data about the absent student as he had done with Cartland. All the students knew that he knew, in the same astounding detail, the same basic biographical detail about each of them.

When he had completed the roll with 'Zygotski?' 'Here, sir!', he looked the the students with a wry smile and said

'That means Cartland, Chapman, Harkstone, Hughes, Luxmore, Mears, and Wilsby are absent . . . I'll make a note of that sometime!!'

And so saying, he turned and left the room in a stunned silence.

To the enthralled student it was one of those moments where a life's 'Impossible Dream' became possible: the dream of training his memory so that it could, in a multitude of special situations, function perfectly.

To be able to remember the names and dates of birth and death and all the important facts about the major artists, composers, writers and other 'greats'!

To be able to remember languages!

To be able to remember the giant catalogues of data from biology and chemistry!

To be able to remember any list he wanted!

To be able to remember like that Professor!

He hounded the Professor for two months until he was finally given the first basic lessons in what he was later to learn were the mnemonic techniques developed by the Greeks.

For the next 20 years he devoured everything he could on memory, creativity and the nature of the human brain, with the vision constantly in mind of a New Super System: a giant, enjoyable and easy to use, super-matrix memory system that would act as a data base allowing everyone to have immediate access to whatever major information structures were important to them.

After 25 years, the New System emerged.

The enthralled student was me.

The one to whom I offer it, with delight, is You.

The Approach

To start you on what will probably be one of the major intellectual and mental adventures of your life, the first section of the book has been structured to give you background information, and to lead you step by step to the Self-Enhancing Master Memory Matrix.

First you will be shown how Memory (mnemonic) Systems started with the Ancient Greeks, and how they were developed to the current day.

Next you will be introduced to the Memory Principles, which will give you the building blocks with which to structure your newly enhanced memory skills. This will be combined with a concomitant development of all your senses.

Following this you will be introduced to the most updated modern brain research, especially that involving the left and right cerebral cortex and the relationships between the upper mid- and hind-brain. Here you will find how the Memory Principles link to our modern knowledge of how your brain works.

Armed with the knowledge of how the Principles work, of how your senses can be enhanced, and of how your brain skills can be used appropriately, you will be given examples of how to apply the Principles. These will be developed into two basic systems, the Link System and the Peg Systems, which will be used to help you memorise the Planets of the Solar System, and basic lists of ten items.

From this you will be taken to the first significant Memory System – the Major System. It is this system that has been used by most of the world's top mnemonists and memory performers. The Major System allows you instantaneously to remember 100 items.

The step from 100 to 10,000 may seem like an impossible dream. To show you that it is *completely* possible, you will be guided through recent experiments to prove that your brain can remember not only 10,000 items but even more with incredible accuracy.

These experiments will be supplemented with information about some of the great brains in history, with examples of their memory feats. Their brains were the same as yours; they simply knew how to use them in the manner outlined in *Master Your Memory.*

By this stage you will be ready and capable of absorbing comfortably the Self-Enhancing Master Memory Matrix (SEM^3). Having mastered the matrix, you will then be able to attach to it all the significant lists of information you will ever wish to know. In the very act of so doing you will be making your 'memory muscle' even stronger, and you will also be increasing your powers of concentration and creativity.

We begin with the Memory Foundations and Principles.

CHAPTER TWO

MEMORY – THE FOUNDATIONS AND PRINCIPLES

The Background

Before modern brain science had revealed, neurophysiologically and psychologically, the extraordinary power and potential of the human brain, the Greeks had discovered that mental performance could be enhanced enormously if certain techniques were used.

The Greeks developed fundamental memory systems called mnemonics, a name derived from their worship of the Goddess of Memory, Mnemosyne.

These mnemonic techniques were exchanged between the intellectual elite of the time, and were used to perform prodigious feats of memory in public that gained the performers personal, economic, political and military power.

The Greeks were thus Gladiators of the Mind, their stadiums being intellectual amphitheatres, and their prime weapon Memory. They would hurl questions at each other concerning the number, names and order of the Greek City States, and the exact phrasing of quotes from their great literature and points of law.

Those who won would become the Senators, the heroes, and the social leaders.

The techniques were based on fundamental principles that were, while being both easy and enjoyable to apply, profound in their effect on memory improvement:

The Memory Principles

The Greeks discovered, by introspection, discussion, and exchange, that memory was in major part an ASSOCIATIVE process; that memory worked by linking things together. For example, as soon as your brain registers the word 'apple' it would remember (link) the colours, tastes, textures, and smells of that fruit, as well as the experiences, friends and occasions connected with it.

The Greeks further discovered that these associations, these links, could be made stronger and more long-lasting if certain basic principles were applied.

There are twelve major memory principles, and they themselves can be memorised by using another memory device: the anagram. If you take the first letter of each of the following twelve key Memory Principle words, you will find they make the phrase 'SMASHIN' SCOPE'. This is appropriate, because applying the twelve principles does give a 'smashin' scope' to thc vista of your memory.

1 SYNAESTHESIA/SENSUALITY Synaesthesia refers to the blending of the senses. Most of the great 'natural' memorisers, and all of the great mnemonists developed an increased sensitivity in each of their senses, and then blended these senses to produce enhanced recall. In developing the memory it was found to be essential to sensitise increasingly and train regularly your:

a) Vision
b) Hearing
c) Sense of smell
d) Taste
e) Touch
f) Kinaesthesia – your awareness of bodily position and movement in space.

2 MOVEMENT In any mnemonic image, movement adds another giant range of possibilities for your brain to 'link in' and thus remember. As your images move, make them three dimensional.

3 ASSOCIATION Whatever you wish to memorise, make sure you associate or link it to something stable in your mental environment, i.e. Pegs System – one = paintbrush.

4 SEXUALITY We all have a good memory in this area. Use it!

5 HUMOUR The more funny, ridiculous, absurd and surreal you make your images, the more outstandingly memorable they will be. Have fun with your memory.

6 IMAGINATION Einstein said, 'Imagination is more important than knowledge. For knowledge is limited, whereas imagination embraces the entire world, stimulating progress, giving birth to evolution.' The more you apply your imagination to memory, the better your memory will be.

7 NUMBER Numbering adds specificity and efficiency to the principle of order and sequence.

8 SYMBOLISM Substituting a more meaningful image for a more normal or boring image increases the probability of recall.

9 COLOUR Where appropriate, and whenever possible, use the full range of the rainbow, to make your ideas more 'colourful' and therefore more memorable.

10 ORDER AND/OR SEQUENCE In combination with the other principles, order and/or sequence allows for much more immediate reference, and increases the brain's possibilities for 'random access'.

11 POSITIVITY In most instances positive and pleasant images were found to be better for memory purposes, because they made the brain *want* to return to the images. Certain negative images, even though applying all the principles above, and though in and of themselves 'memorable' could be blocked by the brain because it found the prospect of returning to such images unpleasant.

12 EXAGGERATION In all your images, exaggerate size, shape, and sound.

Modern Confirmation of the Greeks

Recent brain research, especially in the area of the left and right cerebral cortex, has confirmed that each one of us has, distributed throughout the most evolutionarily advanced part of our brain, an enormous range of mental skills that simply require appropriate training and development for them to manifest and grow. These 'left and right cortical skills' include the following:

1 Words
2 Order
3 Sequence
4 Number
5 Lists

6 Linearity
7 Analytical ability
8 Rhythm
9 Colour
10 Imagination
11 Re-creation
12 Dimension
13 Spacial awareness
14 Gestalt (whole picture)

In the hind and mid-brain, and distributed in part throughout the upper brain, exist your additional mental abilities to:

1 See
2 Hear
3 Smell
4 Taste
5 Touch
6 Move in dimensional space
7 Respond
8 Emote

A quick check confirms the extraordinary similarity between what the Greeks discovered by self-analysis and practice, and what modern science has discovered through the elegant rigours of the Scientific Method.

Armed with this double confirmation, it is possible to apply the Memory Principles with greater confidence and greater efficiency, guaranteeing improvements in your memory and general mental performance that once were considered Utopian.

Putting the Memory Principles to Work

It is advisable to apply the mnemonic techniques to areas where you have been presented regularly with certain information, and having regularly attempted to memorise it have regularly failed. In this way, the technique's immediate value and advantage can be seen.

One such area concerns the Planets of the Solar System.

In the last five years I have researched this memory area

extensively, and have found that in an audience of a thousand people, the following statistics apply:

1 900 people out of 1,000 have learnt and at some time memorised the Planets.
2 In each individual's lifetime, they have been 'exposed' to this information, either in school, or through the various forms of media, for a total number of hours ranging between 10 and 100.
3 100 out of 1,000 *think* they know how many Planets there are in the Solar System.
4 40 out of 1,000 know they know how many.
5 20 *think* they know the order of the Planets from the Sun to the farthest Planet.
6 10 out of 1,000 would be willing to bet on it!

The reason for this staggering loss of knowledge lies in the fact that most of the Memory Principles were not applied when the information was first given.

Check your own knowledge and experience in this particular memory task:

Did you learn the Planets of the Solar System, and if so, how many times and over what period of time?

Do you know the currently accepted number of Planets in the Solar System.

Do you know their names?

Do you know the normal order of the Planets in the Solar System?

Memorising the Planets of the Solar System

Now that you have learnt the Foundations and Memory Principles from both the Greeks and modern brain research, you are going to apply them to the Planets of the Solar System, and thus practise and prepare yourself for using the Self-Enhancing Master Memory Matrix.

There are nine Planets.

In order from the Sun, they are:

1 Mercury (small)
2 Venus (small)

MERCURY (1)

VENUS (2)

EARTH (3)

MARS (4)

JUPITER (5)

SATURN (6)
URANUS (7)

NEPTUNE (8)

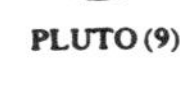
PLUTO (9)

3 Earth (small)
4 Mars (small)
5 Jupiter (big)
6 Saturn (big)
7 Uranus (big)
8 Neptune (big)
9 Pluto (small)

In order to memorise the Planets *for life*, you simply apply the appropriate Memory Principles, creating in your imagination a linked and fantastic story. If you follow it carefully and completely, it will be harder for you to forget than to remember!

Imagine that over the space in front of where you are currently reading, hangs a giant thermometer, and that the sun heats it until, suddenly, the glass containing the silvery measuring liquid bursts and covers the floor and furniture around you with tiny (because the Planet is small) balls of that liquid metal: **MERCURY**.

Rushing in to see what has happened comes an incredibly beautiful, scantily clad, little (because the Planet is small) exquisitely perfumed goddess whose name is: **VENUS**.

You focus so intently on Venus with all your senses, that she becomes almost a living physical reality in front of you. You see Venus play like a child with the scattered mercury, and finally manage to pick up one of the mercury globules. She is so delighted that she throws it in a giant arc, which you see as light glistens off it throughout its journey, until it lands in your garden with a gigantic 'thump'!, which you both hear and feel as a bodily vibration. And on what planet is your garden?: **EARTH**.

Because of the power of her throw, and the height of the arc, when the globule lands it creates a small crater which sprays earth (EARTH) into your neighbour's garden.

Your neighbour, a little man (because the Planet is small) becomes unreasonably angry about the event, and charges out into the garden brilliantly red faced (because the Planet is red) astoundingly angry, and in a mood for total war. The God of War is your fourth Planet: **MARS**.

Just as Mars is about to attack you, you are saved. For

striding on to the scene comes a giant so large and powerful that he shakes the very foundations (and you must *feel* them) of where you are. See him standing a hundred feet tall, and make him as real as you made Venus. He tells Mars to calm down, which Mars immediately does, for this new giant is your friend as well as being the king of the Gods, the fifth Planet: **JUPITER**.

As you look up to the hundred foot high Jupiter, you see the word SUN emblazoned in flashing gold letters across his enormous chest. Each of these gigantic letters stands for the first letter of each of the next three big Planets of the Solar System: **SATURN, URANUS, NEPTUNE**.

Sitting on Jupiter's head, barking his little heart out with humour because he thinks the episode has been so hilarious, is a little (little because the Planet is small) Walt Disney dog by the name of: **PLUTO**.

Re-run this fantasy in your mind, and then see how difficult it is to forget!

In the continuing studies of people's memorisation of the Planets, it was found that before memorising them with the Memory Principles:

a) 800 out of 1,000 people didn't really care about the Planets and seldom paid attention to information about them.
b) 100 out of 1,000 felt interested in the Planets.
c) 100 out of 1,000 were actively disinterested and/or disliked the Planets!

After memorising the Planets with the Memory Principles and Link System, virtually every one of the 1,000 became actively interested.

This on-going study illustrates the very significant fact that if the human brain receives data that is rapidly forgotten or becomes confused, it will reject further data in that subject area. As time progresses, the more and more information that is presented to the brain in the given area, the more it will block that information and will learn increasingly less, often eventually blocking the information altogether.

If the brain, on the other hand, has information in an organised and memorable matrix, each new bit of information will automatically link to the existing information, naturally building into the patterns of recognition, under-standing and memory that we call knowledge.

For example, if you hear that a space probe has been sent to Venus, and you do not know where Venus lies within the Solar System, the first thing your brain will be confronted with is confusion. You will not know which way the probe has gone from the Earth, whether Venus is hot or cold, what its relationship is to the Sun and why anyone should send a space probe there in the first place. As a consequence, you will react by basically rejecting the information.

If, on the other hand, you *know* that Venus is the second Planet out from the Sun, and is the one inside Earth's orbit that is nearest to Earth, you will know that as the space probe goes to Venus, it will be going to a Planet that is nearer to the Sun and therefore hotter than Earth. Your mind will therefore have a mental image of direction, temperature, and nearness to Earth, and will *automatically* make appropriate associations. At the same time as your mind is doing this, it will also be subconsciously, and in many cases consciously, reviewing and confirming your knowledge of the other Planets. Thus, the more you know, *and remember*, the more easily and automatically you begin to know more.

Thus you quickly come to realise that the more structured knowledge you have in your memory, especially if it is in matrix form, the more easy it is to remember more. Your memory is so extraordinary, that once given these basic matrices, it will continue to link on new information to them *without your conscious effort.*

Conversely, if you do not have basic memory and knowledge structures, the more your mind confronts knowledge, the more it disconnects from it, leaving you with a growing 'memory of all that you have forgotten and not learnt'!

Thus if you use your memory well, you may look forward to a life of increasing memory skills, expanding knowledge, accelerating ease of learning, and as a consequence of all these, of both greater mastery and fun.

Advanced Systems

The Mnemonic System for memorising the Planets is a basic Link System. As you progress to the major and super level of mnemonics, the next systems are the Peg Systems, which use a special, permanent and standard list of Key Memory Images, on to which you can attach whatever you wish to memorise.

One of the most basic of these is the Number-Shape System.

The Number-Shape System

In the Number-Shape System, you devise a Key Memory Image for each number, the images acting as permanent hooks for linkage. To create your system, you simply imagine a shape that is similar to or 'looks like' the number. For example:

1 = Paint brush	6 = Elephant's trunk
2 = Swan	7 = Cliff
3 = Heart	8 = Snowman
4 = Yacht	9 = Balloon on a stick
5 = Hook	10 = Bat and ball

Let us say you wished to remember a simple shopping list, in which you wished to buy the following ten items:

1 Oranges	6 A mug
2 Bananas	7 Potatoes
3 Apples	8 Tomatoes
4 Shoe polish	9 Flour
5 Toothpaste	10 Bread

Using the Number-Shape System, and applying the Memory Principles, you would memorise in the following way:

1 You might imagine a paint brush with which you are painting giant, house-sized oranges an even more brilliant orange, as you do so being swamped by the orange smell, and occasionally taking bites out of a giant orange, feeling and tasting the juices that run down your throat and chin.

2 Here you might imagine a swan flying with an incredibly large bunch of bananas in its beak, coming in to land on feet that become banana water skies.
3 In this example you might imagine a gigantic apple tree completely *filled* with delicious, red apples. In this special tree, however, each of the apples is blood red, and is shaped like a heart, and is beating out a strong rhythm as you both look and listen to the entire apple-heart tree symphony in amazement!
4 Imagine that you are on the high seas in your own magnificent yacht, that the waves are rising, that the wind is blowing, and that you are trying to steer the yacht while at the same time getting your shoes 'ship-shape' by polishing them with a particularly strong smelling shoe polish, the smell of it becoming intertwined with the smell of the ocean.

The more you make these exaggerated images for yourself the better, for personal association is virtually always more memorable than that suggested or given by someone else. With the remaining six items, therefore, apply the Memory Principles to the shopping list, making sure that whenever you are in doubt, you add more imagination and more sensuality. Once you have applied the Memory Principles to the memorisation of the list, check yourself, or get someone else to check you. Should you ever miss an item, go back to it, analyse where the weakness was, and strengthen your association.

Creativity and Memory

From the theory you have understood and the exercises you have already completed on the memorisation of the Planets and the Shopping List, the incredibly close link between memory *properly practised* and creativity will be starting to become clear.

The prime engine of your creativity is your IMAGINATION. The creative genius goes on imaginative journeys, taking him/herself into original and previously unexplored realms. There, new ASSOCIATIONS give rise to the new realisations that the world calls the creative breakthroughs – the works of mental genius that can shift the course of history.

So it was with Leonardo da Vinci, Darwin, Archimedes, Newton, Cezanne and Einstein.

Thus it becomes clear that memory is the use of imagination and association to hold the past in its appropriate place and to reCREATE the past in the present; whereas creativity is the use of imagination and association to plant the present thought in the future, and to reCREATE the present thought, whether it be a poem, a symphony, a scientific relation, a building, or a spaceship, in some future time.

The important point here is that, although the name and purposes may be slightly different, the *underlying principles* of IMAGINATION and ASSOCIATION are identical. Therefore, whenever you are practising or applying memory techniques, you are *at the same time* practising and enhancing your powers of creativity.

Memory Systems are not 'Tricks'

Because they are so incredibly effective, and because in recent centuries we have tended to denegrate the brain's abilities, many people thought that the memory systems must in some way be 'unreal' or 'not natural' and therefore some form of trick. Our new knowledge of the function of the brain and memory has shown us that the reverse of what we had thought is true: that our 'normal' way of using our memories is unnatural and counter-productive, and that the initial realisations of early civilisations, such as the Greeks, were indeed the appropriate and *natural* first steps towards unlocking the limitless powers and vaults of our memories.

Increasingly Advanced Systems

From these basic Link and Peg Systems, the early practitioners of memory realised that far more advanced and sophisticated systems could be developed (for further Peg Systems see *Use Your Memory* by the author, BBC Publications), and that the memorisation of much more complicated data could be made as easy as the memorisation of the Planets and a shopping list. One of the most successful of all such systems was the Major System, which is outlined in the next chapter.

CHAPTER THREE

THE MAJOR SYSTEM

The Major System was devised in the mid-seventeenth century by Stanislaus Mink von Wennsshein. Von Wennsshein's objective was to create a memory system that would convert numbers into letters and letters into numbers, thus allowing the memoriser to make words out of any combination of numbers, and numbers out of any combination of letters.

One of the major applications of this was devising a Peg System, similar to the Number-Shape System, but extending not only from 1 to 10, but from 1 to 100.

In the eighteenth century the system was modified and improved by an Englishman, Dr Richard Grey.

In converting numbers to letters, the Major System has a special code, devised so that by its very nature it allows itself to be memorised. The code is as follows:

SPECIAL CODE

Numbers		Associated Letters
0	=	s, z, soft c
1	=	d, t, th
2	=	n
3	=	m
4	=	r
5	=	l
6	=	j, sh, soft ch, dg, soft g
7	=	k, hard ch, hard c, hard g, ng, qu
8	=	f, v
9	=	b, p

The vowels a, e, i, o, u and the letters h, w and y do not have numbers associated with them and are used simply as 'blanks' or fillers in the Key Memory Image Words you will soon be creating.

The Major System's special code can be memorised by applying the Memory Principles to themselves in the following way:

Memorising the Major System Code

0 The letter s, or z, is the first sound of the word zero; o is the last letter.
1 The letters d and t have one downstroke.
2 The letter n has two downstrokes.
3 The letter m has three downstrokes.
4 The letter r is the last letter in the word four.
5 The letter l can be thought of as either the Roman numeral for 50 or a hand with five spread fingers, the index finger and thumb forming an L shape.
6 The letter j is the mirror image of 6.
7 The letter k, when seen as a capital, contains three number 7s.
8 The letter f, when handwritten, has two loops, similar to the number 8.
9 The letters b and p are the mirror image of 9.

Once you have grasped the Special Code, it is possible to translate any number into any word and vice versa.

You do this by decoding the number into its appropriate letters. Once you have the letters in order, you use the vowels and the letters h, w and y, which do not have any number-equivalent, as 'fillers' to help you make meaningful words.

For example, the number 43 translates to the letters r and m. Using one of the vowel 'fillers' (and in devising the system it is always best to try 'a' before 'e', 'e' before 'i', etc because doing it in this way will always enable you to 'get it back' more rapidly and efficiently should you 'lose' the word) you discover the word 'ram', which immediately translates back to the number 43.

Similarly, the number 82 translates to the letters 'f' and 'n'. Again using the vowel 'filler' you immediately have the word 'fan', which itself translates back to the number 82.

Memorising Dates, Phone and Code Numbers

Using the Major System, you are thus able to translate any number (including phone numbers) or any date into meaningful words or phrases that make those numbers or dates simple and easy to recall at your convenience. (See *Use Your Memory*).

Of equal importance, and what is to be the main focus of the remainder of Master Your Memory, is the fact that the Major System allows the brain to develop the system similar to the number shape system, but enabling you to generate 100 key memory images, on which you can then link whatever 100 items you wish to memorise. And from this new base of 100, to leap to 1,000, 10,000 and infinity!

The Major System One Hundred

Following is the Basic One Hundred.

The Basic One Hundred are presented for you in a matrix form to enable you instantaneously to check in groups of tens, and to observe the patterns that ripple through the entire system, in many ways making it even more easy to memorise.

As you memorise the Basic One Hundred, make sure that you regularly refer back, in your mind's eye, to the Special Code, and that each word in your Basic One Hundred has an especially clear *image* that in itself incorporates as many of the Memory Principles as possible.

If, after continual practice, you note that a particular word is causing you difficulty, and that a different word using the same key letters is constantly imaging itself in your mind, feel free to use the word which your own mind recalls more easily.

To assist you in the memorisation of the more rare words in the Basic One Hundred, the word Ra (4) refers to the straw raft/boat that the explorer Thor Heyerdahl used to prove that earlier civilisations could have travelled the major oceans; Dab (19) a flat fish like a sole; Nan (22) (alternate) a large flat Indian bread; Fife (88) is a small shrill flute used with a drum in military music.

	0	1	2	3	4	5	6	7	8	9
0–9	Zoo	Day	Noah	Ma	Ra	Law	Jaw	Key	Fee	Bay
10–19	Daze	Dad	Dan	Dam	Dare	Dale	Dash	Deck	Daffy	Dab
20–29	Nasa	Net	Nan	Name	Nero	Nail	Nash	Nag	Navy	Nab
30–39	Mace	Mat	Man	Ma'am	Mare	Mail	Mash	Mac	Mafia	Map
40–49	Race	Rat	Ran	Ram	Rare	Rail	Rash	Rack	Rafia	Rap
50–59	Lace	Lad	Lane	Lamb	Lair	Lily	Lash	Lake	Laugh	Lab
60–69	Chase	Chat	Chain	Chime	Chair	Chill	Chacha	Check	Chaff	Chap
70–79	Case	Cat	Can	Cameo	Car	Call	Cash	Cake	Café	Cab
80–89	Face	Fat	Fan	Fame	Fair	Fall	Fish	Fake	Fife	Fab
90–99	Base	Bat	Ban	Bam!	Bar	Ball	Bash	Back	Beef	Baby

From 100 to 10,000 in One Easy Bound!

Having established the Basic 100, it is now possible, using a system which helps memorise itself, to develop the 10,000 memory system: The Self-Enhancing Master Memory Matrix (SEM^3).

SEM^3 will enable you to memorise not only all the key knowledge data contained in *Master Your Memory*, but *any* list that may be of importance to you. For those of you using the Universal Personal Organiser (UPO) diary system, SEM^3 will also enable you to memorise, should you wish, not only the major events of each year of your life but *every day* of your life!

The following chapter gives you proof that you can do it, explains the Self-Enhancing Master Memory Matrix in detail, and shows you how to use and apply it.

CHAPTER FOUR

THE SELF-ENHANCING MASTER MEMORY MATRIX (SEM^3) THE TOTAL LEARNING MEMORY TECHNIQUE

Is it possible?

Before developing a system for the memorisation of 10,000 items, it is important to find out whether the brain can easily handle such a matrix!

Both research and history indicates that the human brain can handle it with ease.

The Experiments

In 1970, Raif N. Haber reported the following experiment in *Scientific American*: subjects were shown a series of 2,560 photographic slides at a rate of one every ten seconds. The total of seven hours of viewing was split into several separate sessions over a period of days, and one hour after the last slide had been shown on the last day, the subjects were tested for recognition. They were shown 280 pairs of slides in which one member of each pair was a picture from the series they had seen, while the other was from a similar set which they had not seen. On average their recognition, even after such a drawn-out showing, was between 85 to 95 per cent accurate.

A second experiment was performed in which the presentation rate was speeded up ten times, to one image every second, and the results were identical.

A third experiment in which the new high rate of presentation was maintained, but the pictures were shown as a mirror image still produced identically high results.

Haber commented 'these experiments with pictorial stimulae suggest that *recognition of pictures is essentially perfect.* The results would probably have been the same if we had used 25,000 pictures instead of 2,500.'

In a further experiment reported by R. S. Nickerson in the *Canadian Journal of Psychology*, subjects were presented at the rate of one per second, 600 pictures, and tested immediately after the presentation. Recognition accuracy was 98 per cent.

Nickerson expanded on this research, subsequently presenting subjects with 10,000 pictures, making sure that the pictures were vivid (i.e. applied the Mnemonic Principles). With the vivid pictures, subjects were recalling 9,996 out of 10,000 correctly!! When these results were extrapolated, it was estimated by the experimenters that if the subjects had been shown a million pictures rather than 10,000, they would have recognised 986,300.

The conclusion was: 'the capacity of recognition memory for pictures is almost limitless, when measured under appropriate conditions', according to Lionel Standing in his article 'Learning 10,000 Pictures' in the *Quarterly Journal of Experimental Psychology.*

With this evidence, it becomes apparent that the Self-Enhancing Master Memory Matrix, if used in conjunction with the Memory Principles, can be easily handled by your brain. Further evidence from the great memorisers confirms this.

The Great Memorisers

The great memorisers had brains which were the same as everyone else's. They simply used them more effectively.

1 **Antonio de Marco Magliabechi** was able to read entire books, and memorise them without missing a single word or punctuation mark. He eventually memorised the entire library of the Grand Duke of Tuscany.

2 **Professor A. C. Aitken**, Professor of Mathematics at the University of Edinburgh, was able easily to remember the first thousand decimal places of the value of Pi – forward and backward.

3 The American, **Daniel McCartney**, in the nineteenth century, could tell, at the age of 54, what he had been doing on every day since early childhood. He could give the exact

date, and weather conditions during the day, and tell what he had eaten for breakfast, lunch and supper on any given day.
4 **Christian Friedrich Heinecken** at the age of ten months was able to speak and repeat every word said to him. By the age of three he had memorised most of world history and geography, and had similarly memorised Latin and French.
5 **Paul Charles Morphy** was a chess champion who could remember every move of every game that he had played throughout his championship career, including those he had played while blindfolded. His claims were backed up by the fact that nearly 400 of his games were preserved only because he was able to dictate them *long* after the event.
6 **Themistocles** was able to remember the 20,000 names of the citizens of Athens.
7 **Xerxes** was reputed to be able to recall the names of the 100,000 men in his armies.
8 **Cardinal Mezzofanti**, a nineteenth-century linguist, was able to memorise the vocabulary of between 70 and 80 languages, including Latin, Greek, Arabic, Spanish, French, German, Swedish, Portuguese, English, Dutch, Danish, Russian, Polish, Bohemian, Serbian, Hungarian, Turkish, Irish, Welsh, Albanian, Sanskrit, Persian, Georgian, Armenian, Hebrew, Chinese, Coptic, Ethiopian and Amharic.
9 **The Shass Pollak Jews of Poland** were able to remember the exact position on the page of every word in each of the twelve volumes of the Talmud.
10 **Giant religious books** such as the **Talmud** and the even larger **Vedic scriptures** of ancient India were also passed down by memory.

Homer's *The Illiad* and *The Odyssey* are usually described as great creative works, and are categorised as either history, philosophy or literature. From the perspective of the brain and memory, they can be seen as giant memory systems, for that is indeed what they were. Both were designed to be so *structured*, full of *images*, and so *associative* that they would be completely *memorable*.

Knowing that both 'average' brains, when trained properly, and the Great Brains were and are capable of such apparently extraordinary feats, puts the SEM^3 System easily within your reach.

The Self-Enhancing Master Memory Matrix (SEM^3)

The Self-Enhancing Master Memory Matrix allows you, by using the same Memory Principles to expand from 100 to 10,000 as quickly as you can visualise.

Using the Basic One Hundred from the Major System, you multiply this system by 10, giving you a system of 1,000; you then multiply the 1,000 system by 10, giving you a system of 10,000.

To create the list of 1,000 (0–999), you use the Basic One Hundred, repeated in different aspects of your visual senses.

To create the system of 10,000, you once again use the Basic One Hundred in multiple ways, incorporating each of your senses of vision, sound, smell, taste, touch and sensation, as well as basic data from the physical kingdoms.

By creating a system using such elements, you are at the same time using all of those aspects of your brain that feed your memory skills. You are creating a giant mental gymnasium, which will allow you not only to memorise any list you wish, but which will at the same time provide you with on-going mental work-outs that increase every aspect of your 'Mental Muscle' while simultaneously giving you the opportunity for playing infinite games. You construct your Self-Enhancing Master Memory Matrix in the following manner:

Thousands		0–99	100–199	200–299	300–399	400–499	500–599	600–699	700–799	800–899	900–999
100– 999	**Vision**	–	Dinosaur	Nobility	Moonlight	Ravine	Lightning	Ocean	Concorde	Fire	Painting
1,000–1,999	**Sound**	Sing	Drum	Wind	Moan	Roar	Lap	Shh	Gong	Violin	Brook
2,000–2,999	**Smell**	Sea-Weed	Tar	Nutmeg	Mint	Rose	Leather	Cheese	Garlic	Flowers	Pine
3,000–3,999	**Taste**	Spaghetti	Tea	Nuts	Mango	Rhubarb	Liver	Jam	Clove	Fudge	Banana
4,000–4,999	**Touch**	Sand	Damp	Honey	Mud	Rock	Oil	Jelly	Grass	Velvet	Bark
5,000–5,999	**Sensation**	Swimming	Dancing	Energy	Mingling	Warm	Loving	Shaking	Climbing	Flying	Peacefulness
6,000–6,999	**Animals**	Zebra	Dog	Newt	Moose	Rhinoceros	Elephant	Chimpanzee	Kangaroo	Fawn	Bear
7,000–7,999	**Birds**	Seagull	Duck	Nightingale	Magpie	Rooster	Lapwing	Chaffinch	Eagle	Flamingo	Peacock
8,000–8,999	**Rainbow**	Red	Orange	Yellow	Green	Blue	Indigo	Violet	Black	Grey	White
9,000–9,999	**Solar System**	Sun	Mercury	Venus	Earth	Mars	Jupiter	Saturn	Uranus	Neptune	Pluto

100– 999	Vision	5,000–5,999	Sensation
1,000–1,999	Sound	6,000–6,999	Animals
2,000–2,999	Smell	7,000–7,999	Birds
3,000–3,999	Taste	8,000–8,999	The Rainbow
4,000–4,999	Touch	9,000–9,999	The Solar System

For the numbers 100 to 999 you use **VISION** – in other words, you focus on you *seeing* the image you wish to remember as your key memory image. For 1,000 to 1,999 you use **SOUND**, focussing on your *hearing* for each image. For 2,000 to 2,999 you use your sense of **SMELL**, focussing on your memory images of this sense. And so on, for each thousand, using, consequently, **TASTE, TOUCH, SENSATION, ANIMALS, BIRDS, THE COLOURS OF THE RAINBOW**, and **THE SOLAR SYSTEM**.

For each separate 100 of each 1,000, you have a specific Vision, a specific Sound, a specific Smell, etc. Thus, referring to the Matrix on page 32, your specific visions for the separate 100s from 100 to 999 are Dinosaur, Nobility, Moonlight, Ravine, Lightning, Ocean, Concorde, Fire, and Paintings.

For example, keeping 0–99 as your Basic 100 Matrix, and using nine Vision-images to get you from 100 to 999, you would do the following:

101 might simply be a giant dinosaur with its head rising above the horizon next to the sun at the beginning of a new *day*; 140 would be your same dinosaur leading an incredibly noisy, thundering and exciting dinosaur race. Whatever you wish to memorise as your 101st or 140th items would be attached to these SEM^3 images using the Basic Memory Principles.

Moving up in the first 1,000, all still related to the first of your synaesthesia elements, Vision, all items from 700 to 799 would still be the basic code items, but in this instance connected to the image of Concorde. Thus 706 might be Concorde with its bent nose as a giant jaw; 795 could be Concorde with a giant ball for its wheels. Again, any item you wish to attach to these images would be attached using the Memory Principles.

Similarly, for 3,000 to 3,999, each separate hundred in the progression would have a Taste image attached to the basic hundred, in this instance Spaghetti, Tea, Nuts, Mango, Rhubarb, Liver, Jam, Clove, Fudge and Banana.

To enable you to identify and memorise SEM^3 more easily, a matrix of the 100-divisions is on page 30.

To gain access to any number from 0 to 9,999, you use the simple mental process outlined in the section entitled How to Use Your Self-Enhancing Master Memory Matrix (page 34).

When creating your images, which you should do as a game, as well as a mental exercise and mental brain training, make sure that in your key images for each of the different senses, you emphasise the sense. Thus for 4,143, touch combined with damp combined with ram, you obviously see the image of the damp ram, but your main memory device here is to *feel* the wetness of its fur, its horns, its muzzle, and the smell of damp fur.

By using this Self-Enhancing Master Memory Matrix, you will be not only developing a system that enables you to memorise 10,000 items with the ease of Haber and Nickerson's experimental subjects, but you will also be training each one of your sensory areas, which will have a profound and positive influence on all other aspects of your life. This will include a positive influence on your health. Inability to remember, and subsequent frustration and annoyance at that inability, is often a major cause of stress and disease. This in itself creates a worsening memory. By using SEM^3, you will be reversing the trend.

In many ways you will be creating a positive spiral in which the more you practise your memory techniques, the more your general memory will improve; the more you add your knowledge lists to your memory matrix, the more you will be increasing the probability of automatic learning; and the more you do all this, the more automatically *all* of your various intelligences and mental skills will be improved.

The following chapters outline many of the major memory lists which, like the Planets, are supposed to be learnt for life but which are usually forgotten. Once they are learnt, they form giant foundations from which your brain can, with the ease and facility of 'The Greats', continue on its journey to wisdom.

The Superlist chapters are as follows:

5 Artists
6 Composers
7 Writers
8 Shakespeare
9 Vocabulary
10 Languages
11 Countries/Capitals
12 Kings and Queens of England
13 The Human Body – Musculature
14 Elements
15 Red Wines of Bordeaux
16 Solar System
17 Memorising your Life
18 Memorising a Life: The story of Funes the Memorious

The suggested approach to the following Superlists, is to select the ones which you wish to memorise, organise your Self-Enhancing Master Memory Matrix appropriately, and commence the exercise of remembering them. Throughout, apply the Memory Principles.

To assist you with the construction and organisation of your Superlists, the new book *Memory-Vision* has structured each of the 10,000 SEM^3 Key Memory Images, allowing you to place next to them any thing or list you wish to memorise.

From this point on, it is useful to develop a mental set responsive to any matrices you might find that would be useful to you, and to make a habit of memorising at least one new list per year.

Should you wish to remember the matrix itself, the Basic 100 can be used to memorise each of the key words in the matrix, thus further using the system to memorise itself.

To get you off to a good start, it is recommended that you select from *Master Your Memory* at least six of the lists included. This will provide your brain with enough units of organised data to set your 'memory engine' on automatic growth!

How to Use Your Self-Enhancing Master Memory Matrix

MAJOR SYSTEM – BASIC 100

To find the number 46

1) Go DOWN tens column on left to 40
2) Go ALONG 0–9 line to right till under 6

NOTE: All 40 numbers begin with R
6 is sh or soft ch
The word for 46 is RaSH

TENS	0	1	2	3	4	5	6	7	8	9
0– 9							↓			
10–19										
20–29										
30–39							↓			
40–49	→		→	→		→	X			
50–59										
60–69										
70–79										
80–89										
90–99										

Another example:
Find the word for 85
1) DOWN tens column to 80
2) ALONG 0–9 line to 5

NOTE: Letter for 8 is F
Letter for 5 is L
1st vowel that 'fits' is 'a'
word is FaLL

For application and rules see pages 23–25

SEM^3 100–9,999

To find the number 6,374

1) Go DOWN thousands column on left to 6,000
2) Go ALONG hundreds line to 300–399
3) REFER to BASIC 100 MATRIX
DOWN tens column to 70
ALONG 0–9 line to 4

THOUSANDS	0–99	100's	200's	300's	400's	500's	600's	700's	800's	900's
100– 999										
1,000–1,999				↓						
2,000–2,999										
3,000–3,999										
4,000–4,999				↓						
5,000–5,999										
6,000–6,999	→	→	→	X						
7,000–7,999										
8,000–8,999										
9,000–9,999										

So 6,000 – ANIMALS; 300 MOOSE; 74 – CAR
Your memory hooks could be an enormous moose squeezing into a tiny open sports car!

For 2,351?
2,000 – SMELL; 300 – MINT; 51 – LAD
A powerfully minty smelling lad!

or 5,800 – a flying zoo!

CHAPTER FIVE

THE ARTISTS

The great artists have spearheaded mankind's research into the naure of our perception. They have also recorded human history with an elegance at least equal to that of the poets, novelists, dramatists and literary historians. Knowing the names, birthplaces, dates of birth and death, and some of their famous works, places them, as you did with the Planets, in a context and perspective that allows you automatically and continually to learn more about them as you progress through life. Every time you see an advertisement for an art exhibition in future, the images and information pertaining to that exhibition and artist will add to your growing body of Art Knowledge, and will increase your knowledge of this most important area to your continuing advantage.

As Leonardo da Vinci said, if one wishes to develop an all round mind, make sure you 'study the Science of Art, and study the Art of Science'.

In memorising the great Artists, Composers, and Writers, you might, for example, choose SEM^3 numbers from 1,000 to 1,300, if you had already used your first thousand, or if you wished to reserve the 1,000 to 1,999 matrix especially for lists of famous great brains in the different disciplines. Let's assume that Leonardo da Vinci was your number 1,020. Your SEM^3 Key Memory Image is the number 20 (NASA) joined with the Sound-image of Singing.

To remember that da Vinci was a high Renaissance (rebirth) Inventor with one of his famous works being 'Virgin of the Rocks', you could image a rocket ship with da Vinci piloting it, *singing* an opera aria (to remind you that he was Italian), the rocket ship going particularly high, with a little baby by his side helping him at the controls. Your rocket would be going towards an imaginary planet to rescue a young virgin who was trapped in giant rocks. To remember the dates 1452 to 1519, you would take the numbers 4 = R, 5 = L 2 = N; 5 = L, 1 = T or D, 9 = B, and make word images from them that related to da Vinci. For example, *R*enaissance *L*eading *N*aturalist; *L*eonardo *D*a Vinci's *B*urial. Apply these principles and examples to memorising whichever of the major knowledge matrixes most appeals to you.

Each of the major European artists has been categorised in four headings to aid you both in speed of reference and ability to memorise: Name, Principle Work, School, Additional Data.

	Born	*Died*	*Nationality*
1 **Duccio Di Buoninsegna** Principal work: Christ Entering Jerusalem (Cathedral Museum, Siena) School: Sienese, Pre-Renaissance	1255	1318	Italian
2 **Giotto** Principal work: The Deposition (Fresco in Arena Chapel, Padua) School: Florentine, Pre-Renaissance	1266	1337	Italian
3 **Martini, Simone** Principal work: The Annunciation (Uffizi Gallery, Florence) School: Sienese	1284	1344	Italian
4 **Lorenzetti, Ambrogio** Principal work: Presentation of the Infant Christ in the Temple (Uffizi Gallery, Florence) School: Sienese	1319	1347	Italian
5 **Van Eyck, Jan** Principal work: Giovanni Arnolfini and his Bride (National Gallery, London) School: Flemish	1385/90	1441	Dutch
6 **Angelico, Fra** Principal work: The Annunciation (Monastery of San Marco, Florence) School: Florentine	1387	1455	Italian
7 **Uccello, Paolo** Principal work: The Battle of San Romano (National Gallery,	1396	1475	Italian

		Born	Died	Nationality
	London) School: Florentine			
8	**Van Der Weyden, Roger** Principal work: Deposition (Prado, Madrid) School: Flemish	1399	1464	Flemish
9	**Masaccio** Principal work: The Rendering of the Tribute Money (Brancacci Chapel, Santa Maria del Carmine, Florence) School: Florentine	1401	1428	Italian
10	**Della Francesca, Piero** Principal work: Resurrection (Palazzo Cominale, Boreo San Sepolcro) School: Umbrian	1410/20	1492	Italian
11	**Castagno, Andrea Del** Principal work: The Victorious David (National Gallery of Art, Washington) School: Florentine	1419	1457	Italian
12	**Bellini, Giovanni** Principal work: Pieta (Brera, Milan) School: Venetian	1430	1516	Italian
13	**Memlinc, Hans** Principal work: Man Holding a Medal (Museum, Antwerp) School: Flemish	1430/40	1494	Flemish
14	**Mantegna, Andrea** Principal work: Christ Praying in the Garden (National Gallery, London) School: Mantuan	1431	1506	Italian
15	**Signorelli, Luca** Principal work: Pan as God of Music (Staatliche Museen, Berlin) School: Umbrian	1441/50	1523	Italian
16	**Botticelli, Sandro** Principal work: Birth of Venus (Uffizi Gallery, Florence) School: Florentine	1445	1510	Italian

	Born	*Died*	*Nationality*
17 **Bosch, Hieronymus** Principal work: The Garden of Worldly Delights (Prado, Madrid) School: Flemish	1450	1516	Dutch
18 **Da Vinci, Leonardo** Principal work: The Virgin of the Rocks (Louvre, Paris) School: Florentine	1452	1519	Italian
19 **Durer, Albrecht** Principal work: The Four Apostles (Pinakothek, Munich) School: German	1471	1528	German
20 **Michelangelo Buonarroti** Principal work: Sistine Chapel Ceiling (Vatican, Rome) School: Florentine	1475	1564	Italian
21 **Giorgione** Principal work: Fete Champetre (Louvre, Paris) School: Venetian	1476	1510	Italian
22 **Grunewald, Mathis** Principal work: Crucifixion, from the Isenheim Altarpiece (Musee Unterlinden, Colmar) School: German	1470/80	1528	German
23 **Raphael** Principal work: The School of Athens (Vatican, Rome) School: Florentine	1483	1520	Italian
24 **Correggio, Antonio** Principal work: The Virgin Adoring the Christ Child (Uffizi Gallery, Florence) School: Parma	1489/94	1534	Italian
25 **Holbein, Hans (The Younger)** Principal work: Portrait of Erasmus (Louvre, Paris) School: German	1497	1543	German
26 **Tintoretto, Jacopo** Principal work: The Last Supper (Santa Marciola, Venice) School: Venetian Mannerist	1518	1594	Italian
27 **Bruegel, Pieter (The Elder)** Principal work: The Parable of the	1520/30	1569	Flemish

	Born	Died	Nationality
Blind (Museo Nazionale, Naples) School: Flemish			
28 **Veronese, Paolo** Principal work: Christ in the House of Levi (1573 Academy, Venice) School: Venetian	1528	1588	Italian
29 **El Greco** Principal work: Assumption of the Virgin (1577, Art Institute of Chicago) School: Spanish (by adoption)	1541	1614	Greek
30 **Carracci, Annibale** Principal work: Hercules at the Crossroads School: Bolognese, Classical	1560	1609	Italian
31 **Caravaggio, Michelangelo Merisi Da** Principal work: The Supper at Emmaus (National Gallery, London) School: Independent Tenebrist	1571	1610	Italian
32 **Rubens, Sir Peter Paul** Principal work: Descent from the Cross (Antwerp Cathedral) School: Flemish, Baroque	1577	1640	Flemish
33 **Hals, Frans** Principal work: The Women Regents of the Old Men's Home at Haarlem (Frans Hals Museum, Haarlem) School: Dutch	1581	1666	Dutch
34 **La Tour, Georges** Principal work: Adoration of the Shepherds (Louvre, Paris) School: Lorraine	1593	1652	French
35 **Poussin, Nicolas** Principal work: Rape of the Sabine Women (Metropolitan Museum, New York) School: French, worked mainly in Rome, Classical	1595	1665	French
36 **Zurbaran, Francisco De** Principal work: St Francis of	1598	1664	Spanish

		Born	Died	Nationality
	Assisi (Lyon Museum) School: Spanish			
37	**Velasquez, Diego Rodriguez De Silva** Principal work: Las Meninas (Prado, Madrid) School: Spanish	1599	1660	Spanish
38	**Van Dyck, Sir Anthony** Principal work: Charles I of England (The King Hunting) (Louvre, Paris) School: Flemish, worked in England 1632–1640	1599	1641	Flemish
39	**Claude, Gelle (Claude Lorraine)** Principal work: The Embarkation of the Queen of Sheba (National Gallery, London) School: French, Romantic Classicist	1660	1682	French
40	**Murillo, Bartolome Esteban** Principal work: The Immaculate Conception (Seville Museum) School: Spanish	1617/18	1682	Spanish
41	**Rembrant, Van Ryn** Principal work: Night Watch (Rijksmuseum, Amsterdam) School: Dutch	1606	1669	Dutch
42	**Ruisdael, Jacob Van** Principal work: The Bleaching Ground (National Gallery, London) School: Dutch	1628/29	1682	Dutch
43	**Vermeer, Jan** Principal work: The Music Lesson (Queens Gallery, London) School: Dutch	1632	1675	Dutch
44	**Watteau, Jean Antoine** Principal work: The Embarkation for Cythera (Louvre, Paris) School: French	1684	1721	French
45	**Tiepolo, Giovanni Batista** Principal work: Antony & Cleopatra Frescos (Palazzo Labia,	1696	1770	Italian

		Born	Died	Nationality
	Venice) School: Venetian			
46	**Hogarth, William** Principal work: Marriage a la Mode (National Gallery, London) School: English	1697	1764	English
47	**Canaletto, (Giovanni) Antonio** Principal work: The Basin of St Mark's on Ascension Day (National Gallery, London) School: Venetian	1697	1768	Italian
48	**Chardin, Jean Baptiste Simeon** Principal work: Kitchen Still Life (Museum of Fine Arts, Boston) School: French	1699	1779	French
49	**Boucher, Francois** Principal work: The Triumph of Venus (Stockholm Museum) School: French, Rococo	1703	1770	French
50	**Reynolds, Sir Joshua** Principal work: Mrs. Siddons as the Tragic Muse (Huntingdon Library, San Marino, California) School: English	1723	1792	English
51	**Stubbs, George** Principal work: White Horse Frightened by a Lion (Walker Art Gallery, Liverpool) School: English	1724	1806	English
52	**Gainsborough, Thomas** Principal work: Mr. & Mrs. Andrews (National Gallery, London) School: English	1727	1788	English
53	**Fragonard, Jean Honore** Principal work: The Pursuit (Frick Collection, New York) School: French, Rococo	1732	1806	French
54	**Wright of Derby, Joseph** Principal work: Experiment with Air Pump (Tate Gallery, London) School: English	1734	1799	English

	Born	*Died*	*Nationality*
55 **Goya, Francisco de Goya y Lucientes** Principal work: The Third of May, 1808 (Prado, Madrid) School: Spanish	1746	1828	Spanish
56 **David, Jacques Louis** Principal work: Death of Marat (Royal Museum of Fine Art, Brussels) School: French, Neo-classical	1748	1825	French
57 **Blake, William** Principal work: Dante Meeting Beatrice in Paradise (Tate Gallery, London) School: English	1757	1827	English
58 **Friedrich, Caspar David** Principal work: Man and Woman Gazing at the Moon (National Galerie, Berlin) School: German Romantic	1774	1840	German
59 **Turner, Joseph Mallord William** Principal work: Steamer in a Snow Storm (Tate Gallery, London) School: English	1775	1851	English
60 **Constable, John** Principal work: The Haywain (National Gallery, London) School: English	1776	1837	English
61 **Ingres, Jean Auguste Dominique** Principal work: Le Bain Turc (Louvre, Paris) School: French, Neo-classical	1780	1867	French
62 **Cotman, John Sell** Principal work: Chirk Aqueduct (Victoria & Albert Museum) School: English, Norwich	1782	1842	English
63 **Gericault, Theodore** Principal work: Raft of the Medusa (Louvre, Paris) School: French, Romantic	1791	1824	French
64 **Corot, Jean Baptiste Camille** Principal work: Souvenir de Morte Fontaine (Louvre, Paris) School: French	1796	1875	French

		Born	*Died*	*Nationality*
65	**Delacroix, Eugene** Principal work: Liberty on the Barricades School: French, Romantic	1789	1863	French
66	**Millet, Jean Francois** Principal work: The Angelus (Louvre, Paris) School: French, Romantic	1814	1875	French
67	**Courbet, Gustave** Principal work: Good Morning, Monsieur Courbet (Musee Fabre, Montpellier) School: French, Realist	1819	1877	French
68	**Hunt, William Holman** Principal work: The Light of the World (Keble College, Oxford) School: English, Pre-Raphaelite Brotherhood	1827	1910	English
69	**Bocklin, Arnold** Principal work: Island of the Dead (Metropolian Museum, New York) School: Swiss, Romantic	1827	1901	Swiss
70	**Pissaro, Camille** Principal work: The Red Roofs (Louvre, Paris) School: French Impressionist (Landscape)	1831	1903	French
71	**Manet, Edouard** Principal work: A Bar at the Folies-Bergere (Courtauld Institute, London) School: French, Urban Impressionist	1832	1883	French
72	**Degas, Edgar** Principal work: Cafe Concert at Les Ambassadeurs (Museum, Lyon) School: French, Urban Impressionist	1834	1917	French
73	**Cezanne, Paul** Principal work: Mont Saint-Victoire (Museum of Art, Philadelphia) School: French, Post Impressionist	1839	1906	French

		Born	Died	Nationality
74	**Redon, Odilon** Principal work: Silence (Museum of Modern Art, New York) School: French Symbolist	1840	1916	French
75	**Monet, Claude** Principal work: Water Lilies Series (Louvre, Paris) School: French Impressionist	1840	1926	French
76	**Gauguin, Paul** Principal work: Riders on the Beach (Folknang Museum, Essen) School: French, Post Impressionist	1848	1903	French
77	**Van Gogh, Vincent** Principal work: Sunflowers (National Gallery, London) School: French, Post Impressionist	1853	1890	Dutch
78	**Seurat, Georges** Principal work: Bathing at Asnieres (National Gallery, London) School: French, Pointillist	1859	1891	French
79	**Munch, Edvard** Principal work: The Scream (National Gallery, Oslo) School: Norwegian, Precursor of Expressionism	1863	1944	Norwegian
80	**Sickert, Walter Richard** Principal work: The Eldorado, Paris (University of Birmingham) School: Camden Town Group (Post Impressionist)	1860	1942	English
81	**Kandinsky, Wassilly** Principal work: Improvization No. 30 (Cannons) (Art Institute of Chicago) School: Die Blaue Reiter (The Blue Horseman) Abstract	1866	1944	Russian
82	**Bonnard, Pierre** Principal work: Coffee (Tate Gallery, London) School: Intimist	1867	1947	French
83	**Matisse, Henri** Principal work: Red Studio (Museum of Modern Art, New	1869	1954	French

		Born	Died	Nationality
	York)			
	School: Fauve			
84	**Rouault, Georges**	1871	1958	French
	Principal work: The Apprentice (Musee d'Art Moderne, Paris)			
	School: School of Paris, Independent Expressionist			
85	**Balla, Giacomo**	1871	1958	Italian
	Principal work: Dog on a Leash (A. Congere Goodyear, New York)			
	School: Italian Futurist			
86	**Mondrian, Piet**	1872	1944	Dutch
	Principal work: Broadway Boogie Woogie (Museum of Modern Art, New York)			
	School: De Stijl, Neoplasticism, Abstract			
87	**Klee, Paul**	1879	1940	German/ Swiss
	Principal work: Landscape with Yellow Birds (Doetsch-Benziger Collection, Basel)			
	School: Associated with Die Blaue Reiter, Independent			
88	**Picasso, Pablo Ruiz y**	1881	1973	Spanish
	Principal work: Guernica (Prado, Madrid)			
	School: Cubist			
89	**Leger, Fernand**	1881	1955	French
	Principal work: Les Fumeurs (Smokers) (Guggenheim Museum, New York)			
	School: Cubist			
90	**Braque, Georges**	1882	1963	French
	Principal work: Studio IX (Maeght Collection, Paris)			
	School: Cubist			
91	**Lewis, Percy Wyndham**	1884	1957	British
	Principal work: Portrait of Edith Sitwell (Tate Gallery, London)			
	School: Vorticist (English Branch of Cubism/Futurism)			
92	**Beckman, Max**	1884	1950	German
	Principal work: Departure (Museum of Modern Art, New			

	Born	*Died*	*Nationality*
York) School: Expressionist			
93 **Delaunry, Robert** Principal work: Window on the City No. 4 (Guggenheim Museum, New York) School: School of Paris, Orphist	1885	1927	French
94 **Gris, Juan** Principal work: Still Life in Front of an Open Window (Arenburg Collection, Philadelphia Museum of Art) School: Cubist	1887	1927	Spanish
95 **Chagall, Marc** Principal work: I and the Village (Museum of Modern Art, New York) School: School of Paris, Independent Fantasist	1887	1985	Russian
96 **De Chirico, Giorgio** Principal work: Enigma of Arrival (Private Collection, Paris) School: Italian Metaphysical	1888	1978	Italian
97 **Nash, Paul** Principal work: Totesmeer (Tate Gallery, London) School: English Surrealist	1889	1946	English
98 **Ernst, Max** Principal work: Swamp Angel (Macpherson Collection, Rome) School: Surrealist	1891	1976	German
99 **Spencer, Stanley** Principal work: The Murals at Burghclere Chapel School: Independent, Religious	1891	1959	British
100 **Magritte, Rene** Principal work: The False Mirror (Museum of Modern Art) School: Surrealist	1898	1967	Belgian

CHAPTER SIX

THE COMPOSERS

As artists record the visual history of the human race, so the great composers record the aural/musical history. Sound, as the basis for one of your five senses, hearing, is automatically a major memory device. It is also one of the areas of mental skill that is essential for the development of the Master Memory skill of synaesthesia – the blending of the senses for the enhancement of each and the correlative increase in mental skills, especially creativity and memory.

Once you have organised and memorised, using SEM^3, the following list of composers and the major information about them, you will have created a foundation of musical knowledge that will allow your brain *automatically* to build multiple associations around each composer and each composer's music, and to integrate rapidly those into a growing fabric of delightful and spirit-enhancing knowledge.

When you hear for example on BBC Radio 3, that Smetana was originally known for his astounding energy and enthusiasm, that he lost his two children at an early age, and that he ended his life with the most debilitating disease, causing the physical disintegration of his brain, and yet that he still composed and recorded in intricate detail the nature of his decline and the nature of its effect on his memory, you will listen to his music with greater understanding and compassion, and similarly will know more about the historical times in which he lived.

By using SEM^3 in this way, you will be exploring, with the great historical and current musical brains, the human race's search, through the medium of sound, for an increasing understanding and exploration of its own Nature of Being.

	Born	Died	Nationality	Era
1 **Philippe de Vitry** Famous works: Impudenter circumivi/ Virtutibus Style: Secular and of the Arts Nova	1291	1361	French	Middle Ages
2 **Guillaume de Machaut** Famous works: Messe de Notre Dame Style: Sacred and secular Notes: Well-respected statesman, cleric and poet	1300	1377	French	Middle Ages
3 **Francesco Landini** Famous works: Ecco la primavera Style: Secular Notes: Blind from childhood	1325	1397	Italian	Middle Ages
4 **John Dunstable** Famous works: O Rosa Bella Style: Sacred and secular Notes: Well known for 'singability' of his music	1390	1453	English	Middle Ages
5 **Guillaume Dufay** Famous works: Se la face ay pale Style: Sacred and secular	1400	1474	Franco-Flemish	Renaissance
6 **Gilles de Bins Binchois** Famous works: Filles a marier Style: Sacred and secular	1400	1460	Franco-Flemish	Renaissance
7 **Johannes Ockeghem** Famous works: Missa cuiusvi toni Style: Sacred and secular	1410	1497	Franco-Flemish	Renaissance

		Born	Died	Nation ality	Era
8	**Josquin Desprez** Famous works: Ave Maria Style: Sacred and secular	1440	1521	Franco-Flemish	Renaissance
9	**Heinrich Isaac** Famous works: Choralis constantinus Style: Sacred and secular vocal music	1450	1517	Flemish	Renaissance
10	**Andrea Gabrieli** Style: Sacred and madrigals Notes: Introduced technique 'Cori spezzati' (spaced choirs)	1510	1586	Italian	Renaissance
11	**Giovanni Pierluigi da Palestrina** Famous works: Missa Papae Marcelli Style: Sacred and secular vocal music	1525	1594	Italian	Renaissance
12	**Orlande de Lassus** Famous works: Alma redemptoris mater Style: Sacred and secular vocal music	1532	1594	Franco-Flemish	Renaissance
13	**William Byrd** Famous works: Sing Joyfully/Ave Verum Corpus Style: Sacred and secular choral music, vocal chamber music, instrumental and keyboard music Notes: Described as Father of British Music	1543	1623	English	Renaissance

		Born	Died	Nationality	Era
14	**Giulio Caccini** Style: Le Nuove Musiche	1545	1618	Italian	Baroque
15	**Tomas Luis de Victoria** Famous works: Mass Laetatus Sum Style: Songs in new styles	1548	1611	Spanish	Renaissance
16	**Luca Marenzio** Famous works: Dolorosi martir Style: Secular vocal music and sacred vocal music	1553	1599	Italian	Renaissance
17	**Giovanni Gabrieli** Famous works: Canzon XIII Style: Sacred vocal music, instrumental music and secular vocal music	1555	1612	Italian	Renaissance
18	**Thomas Morley** Famous works: Now is the Month of Maying Style: Secular and sacred vocal music, instrumental music Notes: Specialised in Ballett (light form of madrigal)	1557	1602	English	Renaissance
19	**Carlo Gesualdo** Famous works: Deh, coprite il bel seno Style: Secular and sacred vocal music	1560	1613	Italian	Renaissance
20	**John Bull** Famous works: Fantasia Style: Keyboard composer	1562	1628	English	Renaissance

		Born	*Died*	*Nationality*	*Era*
21	**John Dowland** Famous works: In Darknesse let mee dwell Style: Secular vocal, instrumental music	1563	1626	English	Renaissance
22	**Claudio Monteverdi** Famous works: Madrigals of Love and War, Il ritorno d'Ulisse in patria (The return of Ulysses to his country) Style: Secular vocal, sacred vocal, madrigals, operas	1567	1643	Italian	Renaissance/ Baroque
23	**Thomas Weelkes** Famous works: As Vesta was from Latmos Hill descending Style: Madrigals, sacred vocal and instrumental	1575	1623	English	Renaissance
24	**Orlando Gibbons** Famous works: This is the Record of John, The Silver Swan Style: Vocal and sacred choral, keyboard and instrumental music	1583	1625	English	Renaissance
25	**Girolamo Frescobaldi** Style: Secular and sacred, vocal, keyboard music Notes: Known as 'A giant among organists'	1583	1643	Italian	Baroque
26	**Heinrich Schütz** Famous works: St Matthew's Passion, Christmas Oratorio Style: Secular and sacred vocal music	1585	1672	German	Baroque

		Born	*Died*	*Nation ality*	*Era*
27	**Francesco Cavalli** Famous works: Ercole Amante (Hercules the Lover) Style: Secular vocal	1602	1676	Italian	Baroque
28	**Giacomo Carissimi** Famous works: The Representation of the Body and Soul Style: Sacred musical dramas	1605	1674	Italian	Baroque
29	**Jean-Baptiste Lully** Famous works: L'amour medecin Style: Sacred choral music, comedy ballet, operas, ballets and dance music	1632	1687	Italian	Baroque
30	**Dietrich Buxtehude** Style: Oratorios, cantatas, organ music Notes: Began idea of evening music, public concerts in churches and known as great influence to Bach	1637	1707	Danish	Baroque
31	**Arcangelo Corelli** Famous works: Christmas Concerto Style: Church sonatas	1653	1713	Italian	Baroque
32	**Henry Purcell** Famous works: My heart is inditing, Fantasia upon One Note Style: Secular and sacred choral music, instrumental and keyboard music	1659	1695	English	Baroque

		Born	*Died*	*Nationality*	*Era*
33	**Alessandro Scarlatti** Famous works: Le Teodora augusta Style: Sacred and secular, choral and vocal music, operas, instrumental music	1660	1725	Italian	Baroque
34	**Francois Couperin** Famous works: Concerts Royaux Style: Keyboard music especially harpsichord, chamber music, sacred and secular vocal music	1668	1733	French	Baroque
35	**Antonio Vivaldi** Famous works: Four Seasons Style: Concertos, operas, sacred choral music and chamber music	1678	1741	Italian	Baroque
36	**Georg Philipp Telemann** Famous works: Musique de table Style: Progressive composer	1681	1767	German	Baroque
37	**Jean-Philippe Rameau** Famous works: Hippolyte et Aricie Style: Operas, keyboard music, chamber music and sacred choral music	1683	1764	French	Baroque
38	**Johann Sebastian Bach** Famous works: St. John's Passion, The Well-tempered Keyboard Style: Sacred choral, secular vocal, orchestral	1685	1750	German	Baroque

		Born	Died	Nationality	Era
	chamber music, keyboard music, organ music				
39	**George Frederic Handel** Famous works: Water Music, Music for Royal Fireworks Style: Operas, oratorios, sacred vocal, secular vocal, orchestral, chamber music and keyboard music	1685	1759	German/ English	Baroque
40	**Domenico Scarlatti** Style: Keyboard, sacred choral, instrumental and operas	1685	1757	Italian	Baroque
41	**Christoph Willibald Gluck** Famous works: Don Juan, Orfeo ed Euridice Style: Operas, ballet, songs, sacred vocal music and chamber music	1714	1787	German	Classical
42	**Carl Philipp Emanuel Bach** Famous works: Rondo in E Flat Style: Keyboard, orchestral, chamber and choral music	1714	1788	German	Classical
43	**Franz Joseph Haydn** Famous works: Sturm und Drang Style: Symphonies, keyboard and chamber music, operas, oratorios, choral music	1732	1809	Austrian	Classical

		Born	Died	Nationality	Era
44	**Johann Christian Bach** Style: Orchestral, chamber, keyboard, operas and sacred music	1735	1782	German	Classical
45	**Luigi Boccherini** Famous works: String Quartet in E Major, Opus 13 No 5 Style: Chamber music, symphonies and concertos, opera and sacred music	1743	1805	Italian	Classical
46	**Muzio Clementi** Style: Composed for piano Notes: Known as 'Father of pianoforte'	1752	1832	Italian	Classical
47	**Wolfgang Amadeus Mozart** Famous works: The Magic Flute, Don Giovanni Style: Operas, symphonies, concertos, choral music, chamber music, piano music, vocal music	1756	1791	Austrian	Classical
48	**Ignace Pleyel** Famous works: Sinfonies Concertantes Style: Symphonies, Chamber music	1757	1831	Austrian	Classical
49	**Ludwig von Beethoven** Famous works: Pastoral Symphony, Fidelio Style: Symphonies, concertos, choral music, piano music, string	1770	1827	German	Classical

		Born	*Died*	*Nation ality*	*Era*
	quartets, chamber music, songs Notes: Radically transformed all the musical forms with which he worked				
50	**Carl Maria von Weber** Famous works: The Freeshooter, Invitation to the Dance Style: Operas, orchestral music, choral music, piano music, incidental music	1786	1826	German	Romantic
51	**Gioachino Rossini** Famous works: Barber of Seville, William Tell Style: Operas, sacred choral music, secular and chamber music	1792	1868	Italian	Romantic
52	**Franz Schubert** Famous works: Beautiful Maid of the Mill, The Trout Quintet Style: Songs, orchestral, chamber, piano and operas Notes: Died when only 31 years old	1797	1828	Austrian	Romantic
53	**Vincenzo Bellini** Famous works: I Puritani Style: Vocal, opera, songs and instrumental music	1801	1835	Italian	Romantic
54	**Hector Berlioz** Famous works: Symphonie Fantastique, Romeo et Juliette	1803	1896	French	Romantic

		Born	Died	Nation ality	Era
	Style: Opera, orchestral symphonies, sacred choral music, secular choral music, vocal music				
55	**Felix Mendelssohn** Famous works: A Midsummer Night's Dream, The Hebrides Style: Orchestral music symphonies, chamber music, piano music, sacred choral music	1809	1847	German	Romantic
56	**Robert Schumann** Famous works: A Woman's Love and Life, Scenes from Faust Style: Song, piano music, orchestral, chamber, opera and choral music	1810	1856	German	Romantic
57	**Frederic Chopin** Famous works: The Etudes Style: Piano music, orchestral music, chamber music	1810	1849	Polish	Romantic
58	**Franz Liszt** Famous works: The Hungarian Rhapsodies, Faust Symphony Style: Orchestral music, piano music, choral music	1811	1886	Hun-garian	Romantic
59	**Richard Wagner** Famous works: The Flying Dutchman Style: Operas, orchestral music, songs	1813	1883	German	Romantic

		Born	Died	Nation ality	Era
60	**Giuseppe Verdi** Famous works:Rigoletto, Requiem Style: Operas, sacred choral, secular choral, chamber music	1813	1901	Italian	Romantic
61	**Bedrich Smetana** Famous works: The Bartered Bride, Vltava Style: Symphonic poems, chamber music and opera	1824	1884	Czech-olsolvak	Turn of Century
62	**Anton Bruckner** Famous works: Te Deum Style: Symphonies, choral music, chamber music	1824	1896	Austrian	Turn of Century
63	**Johannes Brahms** Famous works: Hungarian Dances, Tragic Overture, German Requiem Style: Orchestral, chamber music, piano music, choral music, songs	1833	1897	German	Romantic
64	**Alexander Borodin** Famous works: Prince Igor Style: Symphonies and operas	1833	1887	Russian	Turn of Century
65	**Modest Mussorgsky** Famous works: Sunless Style: Operas, orchestral, songs and piano music	1839	1881	Russian	Turn of Century
66	**Pyotr Ilyich Tchaikovsky** Famous works: Sleeping	1840	1893	Russian	Turn of Century

		Born	*Died*	*Nationality*	*Era*
	Beauty, The Nutcracker Style: Operas, ballet, choral music, symphonies, chamber music				
67	**Antonin Dvorak** Famous works: From the New World, The American Style: Orchestral musical symphonies, operas, chamber music, choral music	1841	1904	Czech-oslovak	Turn of Century
68	**Nikolay Rimsky-Korsakov** Famous works: Snow Maiden Style: Operas, orchestral works	1844	1908	Russian	Turn of Century
69	**Leos Janacek** Famous works: The Cunning Little Vixen Style: Operas, choral, vocal, orchestral, chamber music	1854	1928	Czech-oslovak	Turn of Century
70	**Edward Elgar** Famous works: Pomp & Circumstance, Enigma Variations, The Apostles Style: Orchestra, choral, chamber, songs, piano, incidental	1857	1934	English	Turn of Century
71	**Giacomo Puccini** Famous works: La Boheme, Madame Butterfly Style: Operas, choral music	1858	1924	Italian	Turn of Century

		Born	*Died*	*Nation ality*	*Era*
72	**Hugo Wolf** Famous works: Der Corregidor Style: Songs, opera, orchestral, chamber music	1860	1903	Austrian	Turn of Century
73	**Gustav Mahler** Famous works: The Resurrection, Songs of the Wayfarer, The Boy's Magic Horn Style: Symphonies, songs, choral music	1860	1911	Austrian	Turn of Century
74	**Claude Debussy** Famous works: Afternoon of the Faun, La Mer Style: Orchestral, ballet, piano, chamber music	1862	1918	French	Turn of Century
75	**Richard Strauss** Famous works: The Cavalier of the Rose, A Woman without a Shadow Style: Orchestral, operas, choral music, song	1864	1949	German	Turn of Century
76	**Jean Sibelius** Famous works: Tone Poem en Saga, Night Ride and Sunrise, The Tempest Style: Orchestral, incidental, choral, chamber	1865	1957	Finnish	Turn of Century
77	**Ralph Vaughan Williams** Famous works: Pastoral Symphony,	1872	1958	British	Modern Times

		Born	Died	Nationality	Era
	Fantasia on Greensleeves Style: Operas, ballets, orchestral music, incidental, vocal, chamber music				
78	**Sergey Rachmaninov** Famous works: Rhapsody on a Theme of Paganini for Piano and Orchestra, The Bells Style: Orchestral, piano and choral	1873	1943	Russian	Turn of Century
79	**Charles Ives** Famous works: The Circus Band, Three Places in New England, The Unanswered Question Style: Orchestral, choral, chamber and piano	1874	1954	American	Modern Times
80	**Arnold Schoenberg** Famous works: The Blessed Hand, The Transfigured Knight Style: Operas, choral, orchestral, chamber and vocal	1874	1951	Austrian	Modern Times
81	**Maurice Ravel** Famous works: Rapsodie Espagnole, Mother Goose Style: Orchestral, piano, chamber music, song	1875	1937	French	Turn of Century
82	**Manuela de Falla** Famous works: The Three Cornered Hat, Atlantida Style: Opera, ballet, choral and piano	1876	1946	Spanish	Modern Times

		Born	Died	Nationality	Era
83	**Bela Bartok** Famous works: Duke Bluebeard's Castle, The Wooden Prince, The Miraculous Mandarin Style: Operas, ballets, orchestral, chamber and piano music	1881	1945	Hungarian	Modern Times
84	**Igor Stravinsky** Famous works: The Firebird, The Rite of Spring, Orpheus, The Soldier's Tale Style: Operas, ballet, orchestral music, choral music	1882	1971	Russian	Modern Times
85	**Edgard Varese** Famous works: Ameriques, Hyperprism Style: Orchestral, vocal, instrumental and electronic	1883	1965	French/ American	Modern Times
86	**Anton Webern** Famous works: Passacaglia, Das Augenlicht Style: Orchestral, choral, chamber and vocal	1883	1945	Austrian	Modern Times
87	**Alban Berg** Famous works: Wozzeck, Lulu Style: Opera, orchestral, chamber music, songs, piano music	1885	1935	Austrian	Modern Times
88	**Louis Durey** Famous works: Le printemps au fond de la mer	1888	1979	French	Modern Times

		Born	Died	Nationality	Era
	Style: Opera, instrumental and vocal music Notes: One of 'Les Six'				
89	**Sergey Prokofiev** Famous works: The Gambler, War and Peace, Romeo and Juliet Style: Opera, ballet, orchestral, choral, chamber music, piano music	1891	1953	Ukranian	Modern Times
90	**Germaine Tailleferre** Famous works: 6 Chansons Francaises Style: Opera, instrumental and vocal music Notes: One of 'Les Six'	1892	1983	French	Modern Times
91	**Darius Milhaud** Famous works: Les Malheurs d'Orphee Style: Orchestral, choral, chamber and keyboard music Notes: One of 'Les Six'	1892	1974	French	Modern Times
92	**Arthur Honegger** Famous works: Le Voi David Style: Opera, ballet, orchestral and vocal music Notes: One of 'Les Six'	1892	1955	French	Modern Times
93	**Paul Hindemith** Famous works: Matthias The Painter, The Four Temperaments Style: Operas, ballets,	1895	1963	German	Modern Times

		Born	*Died*	*Nation ality*	*Era*
	orchestral, chamber, piano, organ, vocal, choral				
94	**Carl Orff** Famous works: Carmina Burana Style: Cantatas	1895	1982	German	Modern Times
95	**Henry Cowell** Famous works: Synchrony, Hymn & Fuguing Tune, Mosaic Style: Orchestral, instrumental, piano	1897	1982	American	Modern Times
96	**Georges Auric** Famous works: Les Facheux, The Birds Style: Opera, instrumental and choral music Notes: One of 'Les Six'	1899	1983	French	Modern Times
97	**Francis Poulenc** Famous works: A Sonata for Two clarinets, Dialogue des Carmelites Style: Opera, instrumental and choral music Notes: Leader of 'Les Six'	1899	1963	French	Modern Times
98	**Kurt Weill** Famous works: The Threepenny Opera, The Knickerbocker Holiday, The Rise and Fall of the City of Mahagonny Style: Opera, ballet, orchestral, choral and chamber	1900	1950	German	Modern Times

		Born	*Died*	*Nationality*	*Era*
99	**Dmitry Shostakovich** Famous works: The First of May, Leningrad, The Nose Style: Orchestral, operas, chamber music and piano	1906	1975	Russian	Modern Times
100	**Benjamin Britten** Famous works: The Turn of the Screw, A Midsummer Night's Dream, Variations on a Theme of Frank Bridge, Spring Symphony Style: Operas, church, orchestral, choral and chamber	1913	1976	British	Modern Times

CHAPTER SEVEN

THE WRITERS

Writers are more than simply clever users of words. They may be more accurately described as investigators of *all* fields of human knowledge, using words as their major investigative tool. When you explore the world of literature, you simultaneously explore the worlds of psychology, geography, philosophy, history, astronomy, economics, mathematics, politics, biology, physics, exploration, imagination and fantasy.

Thus as you build up your Master Memory Matrix of the great writers, you will be simultaneously extending a multiplicity of associative grappling hooks into all realms of human knowledge. With every author and literary work you come to know, so will your ability to link with every other author and every other work increase. This increase in knowledge will have as its automatic companions an increase in your speed of learning and an increase in your enjoyment of language, literature and life.

		Born	*Died*	*Nationality*
1	**Geoffrey Chaucer** Famous works: The Canterbury Tales Educated: London Notes: Known as the Father of English Literature	1340	1400	British
2	**Edmund Spenser** Famous works: The Faerie Queene, Colin Clouts Comes Home Againe Educated: Merchant Taylors School, Northampton Notes: Writings closely associated with the stages of his life	1552	1599	British

		Born	Died	Nationality
3	**Sir Walter Raleigh** Famous works: The History of the World, The Discoverie of the Large, Rich and Beautiful Empyre of Guiana Educated: Oxford (Law) Notes: Had an enquiring mind and an uncommon literary ability	1552	1618	British
4	**Francis Bacon** Famous works: The Advancement of Learning Educated: Trinity College, Cambridge (Law) Notes: Had unquenchable curiosity about nature of the world and behaviour of his fellow men	1561	1626	British
5	**William Shakespeare** Famous works: Othello, King Lear, Macbeth, Antony and Cleopatra etc Educated: Holy Trinity Church, Stratford Notes: Most prolific period 1604–1608. It is said of him that 'he is not of an age but for all time'	1564	1616	British
6	**Christopher Marlowe** Famous works: The Passionate Shepherd Educated: Corpus Christi College, Cambridge Notes: Died from stabbing during fight with friends while gambling on backgammon	1564	1593	British
7	**Ben Jonson** Famous works: Volpone, Batholomew Fayre, Timber Educated: Westminster School Notes: Leader of new generation of poets known as The Tribe of Ben	1572	1637	British
8	**John Donne** Famous works: Devotions, Elegies	1572	1631	British

Born Died Nationality

Educated: Oxford and Cambridge
Notes: Greatest fame as a prose writer of some 160 sermons

9 **John Milton** 1608 1674 British
Famous works: Paradise Lost, On His Blindness, Il Penseroso
Notes: The Civil War diverted his energies to the parliamentary and political struggle. Wrote Paradise Lost and On His Blindness after he had become blind

10 **John Bunyan** 1628 1688 British
Famous works: The Pilgrim's Progress, Grace Abounding
Educated: Village school, Elstow
Notes: Imprisoned for 12 years for unlicensed preaching

11 **John Dryden** 1631 1700 British
Famous works: Marriage a la Mode, The Rehearsal
Educated: Westminster and Trinity College, Cambridge
Notes: Poet Laureate in 1668

12 **Samuel Pepys** 1633 1703 British
Famous works: Diary
Educated: St Paul's School and Magdalen College, Cambridge
Notes: Diary discovered after his death

13 **Daniel Defoe** 1660 1731 British
Famous works: Robinson Crusoe
Educated: Stoke Newington Academy
Notes: Busiest most prolific time after age of 60; known as founder of English journalism

14 **Jonathan Swift** 1667 1754 British
Famous works: A Tale of a Tub, Gulliver's Travels
Educated: Kilkenny School, Dublin

		Born	*Died*	*Nationality*
	Trinity College Notes: From age 23 suffered from Menieres Disease			
15	**Joseph Addison** Famous works: Cato Educated: Charterhouse School and Magdalen College, Oxford Notes: Member of Parliament for all of his life	1672	1719	British
16	**George Berkeley** Famous works: An Essay Towards a New Theory of Vision, Alciphron Educated: Trinity College, Dublin Notes: First published works were tracts on Mathematics, written in Latin	1685	1753	Irish
17	**Alexander Pope** Famous works: The Rape of the Lock and translations of The Iliad and Odyssey Educated: Self-educated Notes: Suffered from ill-health most of his life	1688	1744	British
18	**Samuel Richardson** Famous works: Pamela, Clarissa Educated: Grew up in poverty, education sketchy Notes: Obsessed with sex, which led to the popularity of his writing	1689	1761	British
19	**Benjamin Franklin** Famous works: Observation on the Relationships of Britain to her Colonies, Rules by which a Great Empire may be Reduced to a Small One Educated: Born Boston, education sketchy Notes: Founded the influential social and debating society (The Junto Club)	1706	1790	American

		Born	*Died*	*Nationality*
20	**Henry Fielding** Famous works: Tom Jones, The History of the Adventures of Joseph Andrews Educated: Eton Notes: Very sick much of his life with asthma and dropsy	1707	1754	British
21	**Samuel Johnson** Famous works: The Vanity of Human Wishes Educated: Pembroke College, Oxford Notes: Recognised that pursuit of learning for its own sake was barren and that it needed to be related to the knowledge of life	1709	1784	British
22	**Thomas Gray** Famous works: Elegy written in a country churchyard Educated: Tutors and Peterhouse College, Cambridge Notes: Letters are among finest in the language, incredible descriptive powers and wit	1716	1771	British
23	**Tobias George Smollett** Famous works: The Expedition of Humphrey Clinker, A Memorable Prophecy of Doctor Smollett Educated: Dumbarton School and Glasgow University	1721	1771	British
24	**Oliver Goldsmith** Famous works: The Vicar of Wakefield, She Stoops to Conquer, The Citizen of the World Educated: Trinity College, Dublin Notes: In his own words, he was mostly addicted to gambling and was an experienced liar	1728	1774	Irish
25	**Edmund Burke** Famous works: The Reflexions on the	1729	1797	Irish

		Born	Died	Nationality
	Revolution in France Educated: Quakers School, Balitore and Trinity College, Dublin Notes: Founded The Annual Register			
26	**William Cowper** Famous works: The Verses Supposed To Be Written By Alexander Selkirk Educated: Westminster School, The Inner Temple (Law) Notes: Unwittingly gave poetry a new direction	1731	1800	British
27	**James Boswell** Famous works: The Life of Dr Johnson Educated: Edinburgh University (Law) Notes: Felt thwarted because he did not attain the political career he wanted	1740	1795	Scottish
28	**Fanny Burney** Famous works: Evelina, Cecilia, Camilla Educated: Self-educated Notes: Her diary is one of the best sources of first-hand portraits of late 18th-century characters and life	1752	1840	British
29	**George Crabbe** Famous works: The Village Educated: Apprentice to a doctor	1754	1832	British
30	**William Blake** Famous works: Songs of Innocence and Experience, The Marriage of Heaven and Hell Educated: Royal Academy at Somerset House Notes: Volumes of meaning expressed in apparently simple musical lines of his poetry	1757	1827	British
31	**Robert Burns** Famous works: Tam-o'-Shanter, Auld Lang Syne	1759	1796	Scottish

		Born	Died	Nationality
	Educated: By his father and mother Notes: Wrote most remarkable cantata, The Jolly Beggar			
32	**William Cobbett** Famous works: Rural Rides, Cobbett's Political Register Educated: Self-educated in the army Notes: His published output was enormous, from farming to politics	1762	1835	British
33	**William Wordsworth** Famous works: Sonnets, Ode on the Intimations of Immorality, Prelude Educated: Hawkshead Grammar School and St John's College, Cambridge Notes: Achieved a remarkable expression of emotions that often lie submerged	1770	1850	British
34	**Sir Walter Scott** Famous works: Ivanhoe, Kenilworth Educated: Royal High School and University in Edinburgh Notes: Wrote almost 40 novels from 1814 to 1832	1771	1832	Scottish
35	**Samuel Taylor Coleridge** Famous works: Rime of the Ancient Mariner, Kubla Khan Educated: Jesus College, Cambridge Notes: Gained knowledge of physiology, anatomy and natural history in Germany	1772	1834	British
36	**Charles Lamb** Famous works: Adventures of Ulysses, Prince Doras, Essays of Elia Educated: Christ's Hospital Notes: Devoted his life to his sister, who was of unstable mind	1775	1834	British

		Born	Died	Nationality
37	**Jane Austen** Famous works: Emma, Mansfield Park, Pride and Prejudice Educated: by her father Notes: Portrayed middle-class society with a remarkable subtlety	1775	1817	British
38	**William Hazlitt** Famous works: The Characters of Shakespeare's Plays Educated: Hackney College, London (Art and Metaphysics) Notes: Ability as a critic with remarkable physical descriptions through his observant artistic eye	1778	1830	British
39	**Thomas de Quincey** Famous works: Confessions of an Opium-eater Educated: Manchester Grammar School Notes: Addicted to opium; work of uneven quality	1785	1859	British
40	**Lord George Gordon Byron** Famous works: Manfred, Don Juan, Childe Harold Educated: Aberdeen Grammar School, Harrow School, Trinity College, Cambridge Notes: Enormous influence on both Europe and England	1788	1824	British
41	**James Fenimore Cooper** Famous works: The Spy, The Last of the Mohicans Educated: Albany and Yale Notes: A judge	1789	1851	American
42	**Percy Bysshe Shelley** Famous works: Prometheus Unbound Educated: University College, Oxford Notes: Died at 30 in a storm while sailing	1792	1822	British

		Born	Died	Nationality
43	**John Clare** Famous works: The Shepherd's Calendar, Poems Descriptive of Rural Life and Scenery Educated: by his father Notes: Known as the Peasant Poet, spent much of his life in an asylum	1793	1864	British
44	**John Keats** Famous works: Hyperion Educated: Harrow and Enfield Academy Notes: Apprenticed to an apothecary, qualified for study of surgery at Guy's Hospital. Extraordinary sensitivity to the impression of the moment	1795	1821	British
45	**Thomas Carlyle** Famous works: Sartor Resartus Educated: Annan Grammar School, Edinburgh University Notes: Lost the use of his right hand and could no longer write	1795	1881	Scottish
46	**Elizabeth Barrett Browning** Famous works: Cry of the Children, Sonnets from the Portuguese, Aurora Leigh Educated: at home Notes: Married Robert Browning. She was recommended as Poet Laureate	1806	1861	British
47	**Henry Wadsworth Longfellow** Famous works: Hiawatha, The Courtship of Miles Standish Educated: Bowdoin, Portland Maine Notes: First poems published at 13	1807	1882	American
48	**Lord Alfred Tennyson** Famous works: Maud, Crossing the Bar Educated: Louth Grammar School, Trinity College, Cambridge Notes: Poet Laureate	1809	1892	British

		Born	Died	Nationality
49	**Edgar Allan Poe** Famous works: The Pit and the Pendulum Educated: University of Virginia Notes: Stories often weird and fantastic	1809	1849	American
50	**William Makepeace Thackeray** Famous works: Vanity Fair, The Virginians Educated: Trinity College, Cambridge (Law) Notes: Travelled the U.S. Died at 52 from heartstrain	1811	1863	British
51	**Charles Dickens** Famous works: Pickwick Papers, Oliver Twist Intermittent education Notes: Often said he wrote about himself in the character of Quilp, in The Old Curiosity Shop. Died of a stroke	1812	1870	British
52	**Robert Browning** Famous works: The Ring and the Book Educated: mostly at home Notes: One of the great romances of literary history with Elizabeth Barrett	1812	1889	British
53	**Anthony Trollope** Famous works: The Warden, Mr Scarborough's Family, The Way We Live Now Educated: Harrow Notes: Clerk in the Post Office	1815	1882	British
54	**Charlotte Brontë** Famous works: Jane Eyre Notes: Taught in Brussels	1816	1855	British
55	**Emily Brontë** Famous works: Wuthering Heights Notes: Died of consumption	1818	1848	British

		Born	Died	Nationality
56	**Walt Whitman** Famous works: Leaves of Grass Educated: Brooklyn Notes: Led a wandering life and did hospital work in the Civil War	1819	1892	American
57	**John Ruskin** Famous works: Modern Painters Educated: by parents and Christchurch, Oxford Notes: Founded the Guild of St George	1819	1900	British
58	**Charles Kingsley** Famous works: Westward Ho, The Water Babies Educated: King's College, London and Magdalen College, Cambridge Notes: Deeply concerned with social reform but opposed to change brought about by force	1819	1875	British
59	**George Eliot** Famous works: Silas Mariner, Middlemarch Notes: Pseudonym for Mary Anne Evans. Read extensively in Theology and Languages	1819	1880	British
60	**Anne Brontë** Famous works: Agnes Gray Notes: Sometimes used pseudonym of Acton Bell. Died of consumption	1820	1849	British
61	**Matthew Arnold** Famous works: The Scholar-Gipsy Educated: Rugby and Balliol, Oxford Notes: Won Newdigate Prize for poetry with Cromwell. Fellow of Oriel College	1822	1888	British
62	**Emily Dickinson** Notes: America's greatest woman poet, always wrote in secret and after her death it was discovered she had written	1830	1886	American

		Born	Died	Nationality
	over 1,700 poems. Her work is considered technically insufficient but flavour of the poetry appreciated			
63	**Lewis Carroll** Famous works: Alice Through the Looking Glass, Alice in Wonderland Educated: Rugby School and Oxford (Maths) Notes: Real name Charles Lutwidge Dodgson, a lecturer in Mathematics at Oxford	1832	1898	British
64	**Mark Twain** Famous works: Tom Sawyer, Huckleberry Finn Educated: Left school at 12 Notes: Real name Samuel Langhorne Clemens	1835	1910	American
65	**Algernon Charles Swinburne** Famous works: Atalanta in Calydon, Aeschylus and Sappho Educated: Eton and Balliol College, Oxford Notes: His poetry often shocked	1837	1909	British
66	**Thomas Hardy** Famous works: Under the Greenwood Tree, Far From the Madding Crowd, The Dynasts Notes: Apprenticed to an architect, he was a novelist and a poet	1840	1928	British
67	**Henry James** Famous works: The Turn of the Screw, What Maisie Knew, The Wings of the Dove Educated: Private tutors and part Law School Notes: Travelled between Europe and America and wrote stories to explain gulf that divided the two cultures. Prolific writer but sometimes difficult for the reader to understand	1843	1916	American

		Born	Died	Nationality
68	**Gerard Manley Hopkins** Famous works: The Wreck of the Deutschland Educated: Balliol College, Oxford Notes: Was an ordained priest and professor of Greek at University of Dublin. Died from typhoid. Felt conflict between poetry and religious calling	1844	1889	British
69	**Oscar Wilde** Famous works: The Importance of Being Earnest Educated: Portora Royal School, Trinity College, Dublin and Magdalen College, Oxford Notes: Leader of the cult of art for art's sake	1854	1900	Irish
70	**George Bernard Shaw** Famous works: The Widower's House, Mrs Warren's Profession, Man and Superman, Pygmalion Educated: Day school left at 15 Notes: Became known as journalist and wrote nearly 60 plays. Letters edited by D. H. Lawrence	1856	1950	Irish
71	**Joseph Conrad** Famous works: Lord Jim, Secret Agent, Under Western Eyes, Chance Notes: Born Polish Ukraine but exiled. Master Mariner in British Merchant Service. Wrote with clarity but never learnt to speak English well. Moralist, was one of the most famous living authors	1857	1924	British
72	**Sir Arthur Conan Doyle** Famous works: Sherlock Holmes Educated: Edinburgh University (Medicine) Notes: A doctor, wrote short stories to supplement his income. Preferred to	1859	1930	British

		Born	Died	Nationality
	write historical romances. Defence of British policy in South Africa won him knighthood			
73	**J. M. Barrie** Famous works: Peter Pan Educated: by his mother, Dumfries Academy and Edinburgh University Notes: The Boy David, his final work, awaits revival so that it can be properly judged in terms of the stage	1860	1937	Scottish
74	**William Butler Yeats** Famous works: Tables of Law, Adoration of the Magi Educated: London, Art School Notes: Encouraged by his father, his Celtic inheritance a powerful influence for him. Founded Dublin Hermetic Society to promote the study of oriental religions and theosophy. Fell in love with Maud Gonne but she refused to marry him – he continued to love her throughout his life. He married another and they attempted 'automatic writing' with striking results	1865	1939	Irish
75	**Rudyard Kipling** Famous works: Love-O'-Women, Kim, Puck of Pook's Hill Educated: United Services College, Devon Notes: Born Bombay, his family moved to London but he was abandoned when his parents returned to India. Kipling as a reporter wrote a great deal about soldiers in the barrack room or in battle	1865	1936	British
76	**H. G. Wells** Famous works: The Time Machine, Island of Dr Moreau, Wheels of Chance, Love and Mr Lewisham Educated: Normal School of Science, Kensington	1866	1946	British

		Born	*Died*	*Nationality*
	Notes: Mixed scientific journalism with teaching. All inventions done before the twentieth century. Science fiction and fantasy stories side-by-side			
77	**John Galsworthy** Famous works: Forsyte Saga, The Silver Spoon, The Modern Comedy Educated: Harrow School and New College, Oxford (Law) Notes: Used pseudonym of John Sinjohn until after his fifth book. Wrote 31 full length plays	1867	1933	British
78	**(Enoch) Arnold Bennett** Famous works: The Grand Babylon Hotel, Anna of the Five Towns, The Gates of Wrath Notes: Went to work for his father, a solicitor, at 18. Became a journalist and then novelist. Prolific writer	1867	1931	British
79	**Walter de la Mare** Educated: St Paul's Choir School Notes: Pseudonym used, Walter Ramal. Continued to write into his 80s. A poet, a storyteller, a novelist, and a writer for children. Saw no need to look down at children protectively	1873	1956	British
80	**William Somerset Maugham** Famous works: Liza of Lambeth, Of Human Bondage Educated: Kings School, Canterbury and St Thomas Hospital (Medicine) Notes: Storyteller of genius with a sardonic view of human behaviour, anti-romantic and mercilessly observant, with an unrivalled skill in realising the climax of a story	1874	1965	British
81	**G(ilbert) K(eith) Chesterton** Famous works: The Father Brown Stories, The Flying Inn	1874	1936	British

		Born	*Died*	*Nationality*
	Educated: St Paul's School, Slade School of Art Notes: Wrote essays on many famous writers, often as a collaborative effort			
82	**John Masefield** Famous works: Salt-Water Ballads, Reynard The Fox Educated: Kings School, Warwickshire Notes: Went to sea but ill-health determined him to become a writer	1878	1967	British
83	**E(dward) M(organ) Forster** Famous works: The Longest Journey, A Room with a View, Where Angels Fear to Tread, Passage to India Educated: Tonbridge School, King's College, Cambridge Notes: Member of the Apostle Society. Chicago Tribune thought the author was a woman	1879	1970	British
84	**James (Augustine Aloysius) Joyce** Famous works: Ulysses, Finnegan's Wake, Portrait of the Artist Educated: Jesuit School Kildare, University College, Dublin Notes: Ulysses published in serial form but was stopped as obscene material	1882	1941	Irish
85	**Ezra (Weston Loomis) Pound** Famous works: The Spirit of Romance Educated: University of Pennsylvania and Hamilton College, N.Y. Notes: Travelled to Europe and was away from America for 40 years. Placed in an asylum but was visited and supported by most of the well-known writers and intellects of the time	1885	1972	American
86	**D(avid) H(erbert) Lawrence** Famous works: The White Peacock, Sons and Lovers, Lady Chatterley's Lover	1885	1930	British

		Born	Died	Nationality
	Educated: Nottingham High School Notes: Tried to interpret emotion on a deeper level of consciousness. Disharmony of home and parents strongly affected him			
87	**Edith Louise Sitwell** Famous works: Facade (set to music by William Walton), Gold Coast Customs Educated: at home Notes: One of most celebrated of English women, awarded four honorary doctorates	1887	1965	British
88	**T(homas) S(tearns) Eliot** Famous works: The Waste Land, The Four Quartets Educated: Harvard University and Merton College, Oxford Notes: The term 'Old Possum' was Ezra Pound's nickname for Eliot and referred to his soft-footed circuitous approach. Born in St Louis, Missouri, became British subject in 1927	1888	1965	British
89	**(Arthur) Joyce (Lunel) Cary** Famous works: Aissa Saved Educated: Tonbridge Wells, Clifton College, Trinity College, Oxford Notes: With British Red Cross in the Balkan Wars and a District Magistrate in Nigeria. Wrote his first novel at 44	1888	1957	British
90	**Ivy Compton-Burnett** Famous works: Pastors and Masters Educated: Royal Holloway College, University of London Notes: Her books deal with family relationships, objectively and unsentimentally	1892	1969	British
91	**J(ohn) B(oynton) Priestley** Famous works: The Good Companions, Dangerous Corner	1894	1984	British

		Born	Died	Nationality
	Educated: Trinity College, Cambridge Notes: Wrote essays, literary criticisms, travel, fiction, autobiography and over 40 plays			
92	**F(rancis) Scott (Key) Fitzgerald** Famous works: This Side of Paradise, The Great Gatsby Educated: Newman School, New Jersey, and Princeton Notes: Ernest Hemingway is said to have helped him to write The Great Gatsby in France	1896	1940	American
93	**William Harrison Faulkner** Famous works: The Sound and the Fury, As I Lay Dying Educated: University of Mississippi Notes: Won Pullitzer and Nobel Prizes. His novels should be read by anyone who wants to understand the grim and complex era of American life	1897	1962	American
94	**Ernest Miller Hemingway** Famous works: In Our Time, A Farewell To Arms, For Whom the Bell Tolls, The Old Man and the Sea Notes: Completely dedicated to his literary career. Several of the literary greats of his time helped him to realise his talents. Shot himself at home in Idaho	1898	1961	American
95	**Noel Pierce Coward** Famous works: Private Lives, On with the Dance, Hay Fever Educated: Italia Conti Academy – trained for the stage Notes: Sought-after actor and successful playwright. Stage sense unerring and ear for spoken dialogue flawless	1899	1973	British

		Born	Died	Nationality
96	**Evelyn (Arthur St John) Waugh** Famous works: Vile Bodies, Brideshead Revisited Educated: Lancing School, Hertford College, Oxford Notes: Worked as a teacher and a journalist	1903	1966	British
97	**George Orwell** Famous works: Animal Farm, 1984 Educated: Eton College Notes: With Indian Civil Police in Burma, then returned to Europe as a teacher. Vivid commentator on reality of depravation and became increasingly pessimistic about affairs at home and abroad	1903	1950	British
98	**(Henry) Graham Greene** Famous works: The Heart of the Matter, Brighton Rock Educated: Balliol College, Oxford Notes: Novelist, journalist and playwright	1904		British
99	**Cecil Day-Lewis** Famous works: Beechan, Vigil and other poems Educated: Sherborne School, Wadham College, Oxford Notes: Poet Laureate and critic. Under pseudonym Nicholas Blake wrote 20 detective novels	1904	1972	British
100	**Samuel Beckett** Famous works: Malone Dies, How It Is, Waiting for Godot Educated: Trinity College, Dublin Notes: Made France his home. Nobel Prize winner	1906		Anglo/Irish

CHAPTER EIGHT

SHAKESPEARE: THE COMPLETE PLAYS

The plays of William Shakespeare are regarded by many as the most comprehensive and masterful literary works in the English language, if not all languages. From them come an enormous number of the expressions and concepts we use today, and the names of many of the characters have become a major part of our cultural heritage.

Once you have a grasp of the basic plot and characters of Shakespeare's plays, you will be able to understand many other literary works more readily, to grasp more rapidly points being made in conversations, and to refer yourself, with sure knowledge, to Shakespearian events and characters. In addition to this, you will be able easily to unravel the 'who was related to who, in what play, when and where?' conundrums in which so many people find themselves. Rather than subsequently 'giving up' on Shakespeare because he is 'too confusing', you will be like an intellectual Sherlock Holmes already hot on the trail of your informational goals.

One excellent method for using SEM^3 in conjunction with Shakespeare, is to set aside an appropriate section of SEM^3 specifically for Shakespeare, and to memorise the basic plot and character for each play when you are about to see or hear it performed. In this way, what you are memorising will be immediately relevant, will assist you with an understanding of the play by which you are about to be entertained, and will enable the play itself to assist you in the memorisation of itself! On the reverse side of this coin, you will find that using SEM^3 to help you memorise Shakespeare will encourage you to reinvestigate the Bard, thus enhancing your social and cultural life.

1589–92	*1. Henry VI, 2. Henry VI, 3. Henry VI*
1592–93	*4. Richard III, 5. The Comedy of Errors*
1593–94	*6. Titus Andronicus, 7. The Taming of the Shrew*
1594–95	*8. The Two Gentlemen of Verona, 9. Love's Labour's Lost, 10. Romeo and Juliet*
1595–96	*11. Richard II, 12. A Midsummer Night's Dream*
1596–97	*13. King John, 14. The Merchant of Venice*
1597–98	*15. Henry IV, 16. Henry IV*
1598–99	*17. Much Ado About Nothing, 18. Henry V*
1599–1600	*19. Julius Caesar, 20. As You Like It*
1600–01	*21. Hamlet, 22. The Merry Wives of Windsor*
1601–02	*23. Twelfth Night, 24. Troilus and Cressida*
1602–03	*25. All's Well That Ends Well*
1604–05	*26. Measure For Measure, 27. Othello*
1605–06	*28. King Lear, 29. Macbeth*
1606–07	*30. Antony and Cleopatra*
1607–08	*31. Coriolanus, 32. Timon of Athens*
1608–09	*33. Pericles*
1609–10	*34. Cymbeline*
1610–11	*35. Winter's Tale*
1611–12	*36. The Tempest*
1612–13	*37. Henry VIII*

1 The First Part of KING HENRY THE SIXTH

This play recalls the triumphs in France of the legendary soldiers like Salisbury, Bedford and Talbot as they prevailed against the treachery and witchcraft of Joan of Arc, the Dauphin and Burgundy. However, many of the characters, times and facts are distorted, in some cases invented.

The play opens with the funeral of Henry V, and this is disrupted by a quarrel between the Bishop of Winchester and the Duke of Gloucester. Talbot recaptures Orleans and has an encounter with the Countess of Auvergne. Then Henry VI becomes the peacemaker for the quarrel at the start of the play, and Joan's demonic powers are displayed by her ability to provoke Burgundy's defection from the English cause. The play ends with York's capture of Joan and Suffolk's seizure of Margaret of Anjou and Henry's betrothal to Margaret and Joan's trial and execution. The ending is inconclusive which leads you into the remaining two parts.

DRAMATIS PERSONÆ

1 KING HENRY THE SIXTH
2 DUKE OF GLOUCESTER, *uncle to the King and Lord Protector*
3 DUKE OF BEDFORD, *uncle to the King and Regent of France*
4 HENRY BEAUFORT, BISHOP OF WINCHESTER, *great-uncle to the King, afterwards* CARDINAL
5 THOMAS BEAUFORT, DUKE OF EXETER, *great-uncle to the King*
6 JOHN BEAUFORT, EARL OF SOMERSET, *afterwards* DUKE
7 RICHARD PLANTAGENET, *son of Richard late Earl of Cambridge, afterwards* DUKE OF YORK
8 EARL OF WARWICK
9 EARL OF SALISBURY
10 WILLIAM DE LA POLE, EARL OF SUFFOLK
11 LORD TALBOT, *afterwards Earl of Shrewsbury*
12 JOHN TALBOT, *his son*
13 EDMUND MORTIMER, *Earl of March*
14 SIR JOHN FASTOLFE
15 SIR WILLIAM LUCY
16 SIR WILLIAM GLANSDALE
17 SIR THOMAS GARGRAVE
18 MAYOR OF LONDON
19 OFFICER *of the Mayor of London*
20 WOODVILLE, *Lieutenant of the Tower*
21 VERNON, *of the White Rose or York faction*
22 BASSET, *of the Red Rose or Lancaster faction*
23 LAWYER
24 GAOLER
25 SIX MESSENGERS
26 TWO WARDERS
27 THREE SERVANTS *to Gloucester*
28 SERVANT *to Talbot*
29 ENGLISH CAPTAIN
30 CAPTAIN *of Talbot's Army*
31 ENGLISH SOLDIER
32 CHARLES, *Dauphin, and afterwards King, of France*
33 REIGNIER, *Duke of Anjou and Maine, and titular King of Naples and Jerusalem*
34 DUKE OF BURGUNDY
35 DUKE OF ALENÇON
36 BASTARD OF ORLEANS
37 GOVERNOR OF PARIS
38 MASTER-GUNNER *of Orleans*
39 BOY *of Master-Gunner*
40 GENERAL *of the French Forces in Bourdeaux*
41 FRENCH SERGEANT
42 FRENCH SENTINEL
43 PORTER
44 SHEPHERD, *father of Joan La Pucelle*
45 FRENCH SOLDIER
46 WATCHMAN *of Rouen*
47 FRENCH SCOUT
48 PAPAL LEGATE
49 MARGARET, *daughter of Reignier, afterwards married to King Henry*
50 COUNTESS OF AUVERGNE
51 JOAN LA PUCELLE, *commonly called Joan of Arc*
52 NON-SPEAKING: *French Herald, Ambassadors, Soldiers, Goalers, Servingmen, Attendants, and Friends appearing to Joan La Pucelle*

2 The Second Part of
KING HENRY THE SIXTH

In Part 2, Shakespeare does follow history a bit more accurately, and shows a nation's abandonment of the principles of orderly social stratification. For in this play the King is defied by his wife, nobility and people; the rule of law breaks down; justice becomes a victim of whim and ambition; goodness is scorned in families and in the nation; and Christian virtue is seen to be impotent when opposed by vigorous self-interest and violence.

The conditions necessary for right rule are represented by the Duke of Gloucester, Protector of the Realm and Henry VI. All that transpires is in reaction to the positive virtues these two men possess.

DRAMATIS PERSONÆ

1 KING HENRY THE SIXTH
2 HUMPHREY, DUKE OF GLOUCESTER, *his uncle*
3 CARDINAL BEAUFORT, BISHOP OF WINCHESTER *great-uncle to the King*
4 RICHARD PLANTAGENET, DUKE OF YORK
5 EDWARD } *sons of the Duke of York*
6 RICHARD }
7 DUKE OF SOMERSET
8 WILLIAM DE LA POLE, DUKE OF SUFFOLK } *King's Party*
9 DUKE OF BUCKINGHAM }
10 LORD CLIFFORD }
11 YOUNG CLIFFORD, *his son*
12 EARL OF SALISBURY } *York Faction*
13 EARL OF WARWICK }
14 LORD SCALES
15 LORD SAY
16 SIR HUMPHREY STAFFORD
17 WILLIAM STAFFORD, *his brother*
18 SIR JOHN STANLEY
19 VAUX
20 SEA-CAPTAIN
21 MASTER
22 MASTER'S MATE
23 WALTER WHITMORE
24 TWO GENTLEMEN, *prisoners with Suffolk*
25 JOHN HUME } *priests*
26 JOHN SOUTHWELL }
27 BOLINGBROKE, *a conjurer*
28 THOMAS HORNER, *an armourer*
29 PETER THUMP, *his man*
30 CLERK *of Chatham*
31 MAYOR *of Saint Alban's*
32 SIMPCOX, *an imposter*
33 ALEXANDER IDEN, *a Kentish gentleman*
34 JACK CADE, *a rebel*
35 GEORGE BEVIS
36 JOHN HOLLAND } *followers of Cade*
37 DICK, *the butcher* }
38 SMITH, *the weaver* }
39 MICHAEL
40 TWO MURDERERS
41 FIVE MESSENGERS
42 TWO PETITIONERS
43 SPIRIT
44 BEADLE
45 TWO 'PRENTICES
46 THREE NEIGHBOURS TO HORNER
47 SERVANT *to Gloucester*
48 SHERIFF
49 HERALD
50 A POST
51 COMMONS
52 A CITIZEN
53 A SOLDIER
54 MARGARET, *Queen to King Henry*
55 ELEANOR, *Duchess of Gloucester*
56 MARGARET JOURDAIN, *a witch*
57 WIFE *to Simpcox*
58 NON-SPEAKING: *Mathew Goffe, Petitioners, Guards, Servants, Attendants, Citizens, 'Prentices, Officers of the Sheriff, Lords, Ladies and Soldiers*

3 The Third Part of KING HENRY THE SIXTH

The ebb and flo motion of this play seems an accurate evocation of the Wars of Roses. The historical events covered stretch from the aftermath of the first battle of Saint Albans in 1455 to 1475 when a poverty-stricken King Reignier pawned his kingdoms of Naples, Sicily and the County of Provence to King Louis XI in order to pay the ransom demanded by Edward IV for Queen Margaret.

There is a good deal of telescoping of time and fusing of events, many reasons for this having been suggested. The subject of the play is obviously the erosion of all values that people have traditionally shored up against the encroachment of chaos in public life, to follow the remorseless pressures to act that events force upon men.

DRAMATIS PERSONÆ

1 KING HENRY THE SIXTH
2 EDWARD, PRINCE OF WALES, *his son*
3 LEWIS XI, *King of France*
4 DUKE OF SOMERSET
5 DUKE OF EXETER
6 EARL OF OXFORD
7 EARL OF NORTHUMBERLAND
8 EARL OF WESTMORELAND
9 LORD CLIFFORD
10 RICHARD PLANTAGENET, DUKE OF YORK
11 EDWARD, *Earl of March, afterwards* KING EDWARD IV
12 EDMUND, *Earl of Rutland*
13 GEORGE, *afterwards* DUKE OF CLARENCE
14 RICHARD, *afterwards* DUKE OF GLOUCESTER
(11–14: *his sons*)
15 DUKE OF NORFOLK
16 MARQUESS OF MONTAGUE
17 EARL OF WARWICK
18 EARL OF PEMBROKE
19 LORD HASTINGS
20 LORD STAFFORD
21 SIR JOHN MORTIMER
22 SIR HUGH MORTIMER
(21–22: *uncles to the Duke of York*)
23 LORD RIVERS, *brother to Lady Grey*
24 SIR WILLIAM STANLEY
25 SIR JOHN MONTGOMERY
26 SIR JOHN SOMERVILLE
27 TUTOR TO RUTLAND
28 MAYOR OF YORK
29 LIEUTENANT OF THE TOWER
30 NOBLEMAN
31 TWO KEEPERS
32 HUNTSMAN
33 SON, *that has killed his father*
34 FATHER, *that has killed his son*
35 SEVEN MESSENGERS
36 POST
37 SOLDIER
38 QUEEN MARGARET
39 ELIZABETH WOODVILLE, LADY GREY, *afterwards* QUEEN *to Edward IV*
40 BONA, *sister to the French Queen*

41 NON-SPEAKING: *Henry, Earl of Richmond, Mayor of Coventry, Admiral called Bourbon, Nurse; Aldermen, Soldiers, Attendants*

4 The Tragedy of
KING RICHARD THE THIRD

During the reign of Edward IV, Richard Duke of Gloucester and the youngest brother of the King has arranged the imprisonment of another brother, Duke of Clarence. Richard has Clarence murdered, marries Lady Anne, and plans to become King.

When Edward dies, Richard gains control of King Edward V and his brother the Duke of York. He conspires until he becomes King and has the young princes murdered. He then plans to marry Edward IV's daughter Elizabeth.

The Earl of Richmond and his army oppose him at Bosworth. The ghosts of all Richard's victims appear and prophesy his death. Victorious Richmond marries Elizabeth.

DRAMATIS PERSONÆ

1 KING EDWARD THE FOURTH
2 EDWARD, PRINCE OF WALES, *afterwards* KING EDWARD V, *later as a* GHOST — *sons to the King*
3 RICHARD, DUKE OF YORK, *later as a* GHOST — *sons to the King*
4 GEORGE, DUKE OF CLARENCE, *later as a* GHOST — *brothers to the King*
5 RICHARD, DUKE OF GLOUCESTER, *afterwards* KING RICHARD III — *brothers to the King*
6 EDWARD, EARL OF WARWICK, *son of Clarence*
7 HENRY, EARL OF RICHMOND, *afterwards* KING HENRY VII
8 CARDINAL BOURCHIER, ARCHBISHOP OF CANTERBURY
9 THOMAS ROTHERHAM, ARCHBISHOP OF YORK
10 JOHN MORTON, BISHOP OF ELY
11 DUKE OF BUCKINGHAM, *later as a* GHOST
12 DUKE OF NORFOLK
13 EARL OF SURREY, *his son*
14 EARL RIVERS, *brother to Elizabeth, later a* GHOST
15 MARQUIS OF DORSET — *sons to Elizabeth*
16 LORD GREY, *later as a* GHOST — *sons to Elizabeth*
17 EARL OF OXFORD
18 LORD HASTINGS, *later as a* GHOST
19 LORD STANLEY, *later* EARL OF DERBY
20 LORD LOVEL
21 SIR THOMAS VAUGHAN, *later as a* GHOST
22 SIR RICHARD RATCLIFF
23 SIR WILLIAM CATESBY
24 SIR JAMES TYRREL
25 SIR JAMES BLUNT
26 SIR WALTER HERBERT
27 SIR ROBERT BRAKENBURY, *Lieutenant of the Tower*
28 CHRISTOPHER URSWICK, *a priest*
29 LORD MAYOR OF LONDON
30 SHERIFF OF WILTSHIRE
31 GENTLEMAN MOURNER
32 TWO MURDERERS
33 THREE CITIZENS
34 SIX MESSENGERS

35 PURSUIVANT
36 PRIEST
37 SCRIVENER
38 PAGE *to Richard III*
39 GHOSTS OF KING HENRY VI
40 LORDS
41 ELIZABETH, *queen to King Edward IV*
42 MARGARET, *widow to King Henry VI*
43 DUCHESS OF YORK, *mother to King Edward IV*
44 LADY ANNE, *widow of Edward Prince of Wales, son to King Henry VI, afterwards married to Richard, later as a* GHOST
45 MARGARET PLANTAGENET, *daughter of Clarence*
46 NON-SPEAKING: *Lords and other Attendants, Two Bishops, Sir William Brandon, Citizens, Soldiers*

5 THE COMEDY OF ERRORS

Based on Plautus's Menaechmi. A tale of twin brothers, one who wanders away from home as a boy, and the father dies of grief.

The boy lives, grows up, marries and the story begins as he has stolen his wife's cloak to give to his mistress. At the same time his brother arrives looking for his lost twin.

At this point, the mistress mistakes the twin for her lover and the plot becomes wonderfully intertwined with the brother having the cloak, and also meeting his brother's wife. When the original one returns he is locked out of both his lover's and his wife's houses. However, just in time the two brothers are seen together and the reason for the confusion is evident. They are happily reunited and go to live in Syracuse.

DRAMATIS PERSONÆ

1 SOLINUS, DUKE OF EPHESUS
2 ÆGEON, *a merchant of Syracuse*
3 ANTIPHOLUS OF EPHESUS
4 ANTIPHOLUS OF SYRACUSE — *twin brothers, and sons of Ægeon and Æmilia*
5 DROMIO OF EPHESUS
6 DROMIO OF SYRACUSE — *twin brothers, and attendants on the two Antipholuses*
7 BALTHAZAR, *a merchant*
8 ANGELO, *a goldsmith*
9 FIRST MERCHANT, *friend to Antipholus of Syracuse*
10 SECOND MERCHANT, *to whom Angelo is a debtor*
11 PINCH, *a schoolmaster*
12 A SERVANT
13 A GAOLER
14 AN OFFICER
15 ÆMILIA, *wife to Ægeon, an abbess at Ephesus*
16 ADRIANA, *wife to Antipholus of Ephesus*
17 LUCIANA, *her sister*
18 LUCE, *a servant to Adriana*
19 A COURTESAN
20 NON-SPEAKING: *Officers and other Attendants*

6 TITUS ANDRONICUS

This play is academic, ambitious and masterfully planned, with a multiplicity of fearful events and climaxes. It begins late 4 Century AD with Italy being plundered by the Goths. Titus Andronicus raises the siege of Rome, and becomes engaged in a ten year struggle with the Goths. He eventually kills the Gothic king, but the king's sons continue the battle.

The Roman Emperor decides on a political marriage, and the Empress tries to banish Titus. However, the people revolt and the decision must be reversed. The Empress then has a child by a Moor, and arranges the killing of the Emperor's son (by an earlier marriage). Then her sons rape and mutilate the Emperor's son's wife. Titus learns of all this and feigns madness, kills the Empress' sons and, revenge complete, he kills himself.

DRAMATIS PERSONÆ

1 SATURNINUS, *oldest son to the late Emperor of Rome, and afterwards declared* EMPEROR
2 BASSIANUS, *brother to Saturninus; in love with Lavinia*
3 TITUS ANDRONICUS, *a noble Roman, general against the Goths*
4 MARCUS ANDRONICUS, *tribune of the people and brother to Titus*
5 LUCIUS
6 QUINTUS *sons to Titus*
7 MARTIUS *Andronicus*
8 MUTIUS
9 YOUNG LUCIUS, *a boy, son to Lucius*
10 PUBLIUS, *son to Marcus the tribune*
11 ÆMILIUS, *a noble Roman*
12 DEMETRIUS *sons to Tamora*
13 CHIRON
14 AARON, *a Moor, beloved by Tamora*
15 A CAPTAIN
16 A TRIBUNE
17 A MESSENGER
18 A CLOWN
19 THREE GOTHS
20 TAMORA, *Queen of the Goths*
21 LAVINIA, *daughter to Titus Andronicus*
22 A NURSE
23 NON-SPEAKING: *Sempronius, Caius, and Valentine, kinsmen to Titus; Alarbus, oldest son to Tamora; Senators, Tribunes, Soldiers, Attendants, Romans, and Goths*

7 THE TAMING OF THE SHREW

A play about the changing moods of human nature brought about by tricks and deceit. Bianca is not allowed to marry until her bad-tempered elder sister is married. Her father, Baptista, looks for tutors for Bianca and suitors for Katharina.

Lucentio falls in love with Bianca, disguises himself as a tutor, and later they elope. Petruchio, who is prepared to marry anyone for money, takes on Katharina but it is not quite a typical wedding.

Lucentio and Bianco return married and their parents are offended by their secret wedding. Petruchio has tamed Katharina, who is now a model-wife whereas Bianca and Lucentio are not so sure of each other.

DRAMATIS PERSONÆ

1 A LORD
2 CHRISTOPHER SLY, *a tinker*
3 TWO HUNTSMEN
4 SERVINGMAN
5 PAGE
6 MESSENGER
7 THREE SERVANTS
8 PLAYERS
9 HOSTESS
Persons in the Induction

10 BAPTISTA MINOLA, *a rich gentleman of Padua*
11 VINCENTIO, *an old gentleman of Pisa*
12 LUCENTIO, *son to Vincentio, in love with Bianca*
13 PETRUCHIO, *a gentleman of Verona, a suitor to Katharina*
14 GREMIO
15 HORTENSIO
suitors to Bianca
16 TRANIO
17 BIONDELLO
servants to Lucentio
18 GRUMIO
19 CURTIS
20 PETER
21 NATHANIEL
22 PHILIP
23 JOSEPH
24 NICHOLAS
servants to Petruchio
25 A PEDANT
26 A TAILOR
27 A HABERDASHER
28 KATHARINA, *the shrew*
29 BIANCA
daughters to Baptista
30 WIDOW
31 NON-SPEAKING: *Attendants and Servants*

8 THE TWO GENTLEMEN OF VERONA

This appears to have been one of Shakespeare's early 'experiments'. He has extended his range by turning his attention to the technical problems inherent in the dramatisation of materials drawn from the genre known as Romance. There is the subjection of love to strain from without and within.

In Proteus's case his father's command separates him from his mistress, and then he falls prey to a momentary sensual attraction. Valentine's case is his own stupidity and the Duke's decree of banishment. There is also the conflicting desire between the demands of friendship between the men, and their various sexual attractions. In the end Valentine restores Proteus to his own favour and even offers him his own mistress.

DRAMATIS PERSONÆ

1 DUKE OF MILAN, *Father to Silvia*
2 VALENTINE } *the two Gentlemen*
3 PROTEUS }
4 ANTONIO, *Father to Proteus*
5 THURIO, *a foolish rival to Valentine*
6 EGLAMOUR, *Agent for Silvia in her escape*
7 HOST, *where Julia lodges*
8 THREE OUTLAWS, *with Valentine*
9 SPEED, *a clownish servant to Valentine*
10 LAUNCE, *the like to Proteus*
11 PANTHINO, *Servant to Antonio*
12 JULIA, *beloved of Proteus*
13 SILVIA, *beloved of Valentine*
14 LUCETTA, *waiting-woman to Julia*
15 NON-SPEAKING: *Servants and Musicians*

9 LOVE'S LABOUR'S LOST

Ferdinand, King of Navarre, persuades three of his courtiers, Berowne, Longaville and Dumain, to abstain from the company of women for three years but the arrival of a French Princess and her entourage causes problems; as they each fall in love: Berowne with Rosalind; the King with the Princess; Longaville with Maria; and Dumain with Katharine.

Love poems are sent, tricks are played, but news of the French King's death necessitates the ladies' return to France. They promise that after their period of mourning, they will return if, in between, the four men spend that time doing good deeds.

DRAMATIS PERSONÆ

1 FERDINAND, KING OF NAVARRE
2 BEROWNE
3 LONGAVILLE
4 DUMAIN
(2–4: lords attending on the King)
5 BOYET
6 MERCADE
(5–6: lords attending on the Princess of France)
7 DON ADRIANO DE ARMADO, *a fantastical Spaniard*
8 SIR NATHANIEL, *a curate*
9 HOLOFERNES, *a schoolmaster*
10 DULL, *a constable*
11 COSTARD, *a clown*
12 MOTH, *a page to Armado*
13 A FORESTER
14 A LORD OF FRANCE
15 THE PRINCESS OF FRANCE
16 ROSALINE
17 MARIA
18 KATHARINE
(16–18: ladies attending on the Princess)
19 JAQUENETTA, *a country wench*
20 NON-SPEAKING: *Lords, Attendants, Blackamoors, etc.*

10 ROMEO AND JULIET

The Capulets and the Montagues are feuding families of Verona.

Paris has asked to marry Juliet, Capulet's 13-year-old daughter, but is told she is far too young. Disguised at a Capulet party, Romeo, son of Montague, meets Juliet and they fall in love. They get married secretly but Romeo is banished after a family fight in which Mercutio and Tybalt are killed.

Capulet changes his mind and insists Paris and Juliet are married within two days. Juliet takes a potion to give herself the appearance of death, Romeo thinks she is dead and poisons himself. On waking, Juliet kills herself. The tragedy finally reconciles the families.

DRAMATIS PERSONÆ

1 ESCALUS, PRINCE OF VERONA
2 PARIS, *a young nobleman, kinsman to the Prince*
3 MONTAGUE }
4 CAPULET } *heads of two houses at variance with each other*
5 COUSIN TO CAPULET, *an old man*
6 ROMEO, *son to Montague*
7 MERCUTIO, *kinsman to the Prince, and friend to Romeo*
8 BENVOLIO, *nephew to Montague, and friend to Romeo*
9 TYBALT, *nephew to Lady Capulet*
10 FRIAR LAURENCE }
11 FRIAR JOHN } *Franciscans*
12 BALTHASAR, *servant to Romeo*
13 SAMPSON }
14 GREGORY } *servants to Capulet*
15 PETER, *servant to Juliet's nurse*
16 ABRAHAM, *servant to Montague*
17 AN APOTHECARY
18 THREE MUSICIANS
19 PAGE *to Paris*
20 THREE WATCHMEN
21 A CITIZEN *of Verona*
22 THREE SERVANTS *to Capulet*
23 LADY MONTAGUE, *wife to Montague*
24 LADY CAPULET, *wife to Capulet*
25 JULIET, *daughter to Capulet*
26 NURSE *to Juliet*
27 CHORUS
28 NON-SPEAKING: *Citizens of Verona, Maskers, Musicians, Page to Mercutio, Guards, Watchmen, and Attendants*

11 The Tragedy of KING RICHARD II

Mowbray and Bolingbroke are to duel over the murder of the Duke of Gloucester, for which King Richard II was responsible. Richard intervenes but banishes Bolingbroke and Mowbray.

Richard levies various illegal taxes and confiscates the property of John of Gaunt (Bolingbroke's father) on his death. While Richard is in Ireland, Bolingbroke returns to restore his inheritance. He and his supporters march through England. Richard returns and abdicates in favour of Bolingbroke. Richard is sent to Pontefract, where he is murdered by Exton, who presents the body to Bolingbroke. He in turn feels remorse and goes on a crusade to atone for Richard's death.

DRAMATIS PERSONÆ

1 KING RICHARD THE SECOND
2 JOHN OF GAUNT, DUKE OF LANCASTER — *uncles to the King*
3 EDMUND OF LANGLEY, DUKE OF YORK — *uncles to the King*
4 HENRY, *surnamed* BOLINGBROKE, DUKE OF HEREFORD, *son to John of Gaunt; afterwards* KING HENRY IV
5 DUKE OF AUMERLE, *son to the Duke of York*
6 THOMAS MOWBRAY, DUKE OF NORFOLK
7 DUKE OF SURREY
8 EARL OF SALISBURY
9 LORD BERKELEY
10 BUSHY
11 BAGOT — *servants to King Richard*
12 GREEN — *servants to King Richard*
13 EARL OF NORTHUMBERLAND
14 HENRY PERCY, *surnamed Hotspur, his son*
15 LORD ROSS
16 LORD WILLOUGHBY
17 LORD FITZWATER
18 BISHOP OF CARLISLE
19 ABBOT OF WESTMINSTER
20 LORD MARSHAL
21 SIR STEPHEN SCROOP
22 SIR PIERCE OF EXTON
23 CAPTAIN *to a band of Welshmen*
24 TWO HERALDS
25 ANOTHER LORD
26 GARDENER
27 GROOM OF THE STABLE
28 KEEPER
29 TWO SERVANTS *to York*
30 SERVANT *to Exton*
31 QUEEN *to King Richard*
32 DUCHESS OF YORK
33 DUCHESS OF GLOUCESTER
34 LADY *attending on the Queen*
35 NON-SPEAKING: *Lords, Ladies, Officers, Soldiers, Gardeners, Guards, and other Attendants*

12 A MIDSUMMER NIGHT'S DREAM

Theseus, Duke of Athens, is to marry Hippolyta, Queen of the Amazons. Hermia refuses to give up her lover, Lysander, to marry Demetrius, and they flee to a wood, persued by Demetrius, who is followed by Helena, whom Demetrius slighted in love.

In the wood, a lot of tomfoolery goes on with Oberon casting spells on Titania and Puck playing tricks on Bottom.

They all return to Athens for a triple wedding, at which the play Pyramus and Thisbe is enacted. The fairies bless the couples.

DRAMATIS PERSONÆ

1 THESEUS, *Duke of Athens*
2 EGEUS, *father to Hermia*
3 LYSANDER
4 DEMETRIUS *in love with Hermia*
5 PHILOSTRATE, *master of the revels to Theseus*
6 QUINCE, *a carpenter*
7 SNUG, *a joiner*
8 BOTTOM, *a weaver*
9 FLUTE, *a bellows-mender*
10 SNOUT, *a tinker*
11 STARVELING, *a tailor*
12 HIPPOLYTA, *Queen of the Amazons, betrothed to Theseus*
13 HERMIA, *daughter to Egeus, in love with Lysander*
14 HELENA, *in love with Demetrius*
15 OBERON, *King of the fairies*
16 TITANIA, *Queen of the fairies*
17 PUCK, *or Robin Goodfellow*
18 PEASEBLOSSOM
19 COBWEB
20 MOTH
21 MUSTARDSEED *fairies*
22 TWO FAIRIES
23 NON-SPEAKING: *Attendants on Theseus and Hippolyta; Fairies attending their King and Queen.*

13 The Life and Death of KING JOHN

In this play the motives of behaviour of men in conflict for power are explored. There is a concentration of events around the fate of Arthur and the fore-shortening of the time scheme results in a dramatic intensification of the pressures in the conflict. The corrupt greed for power of John is set against the ruthless fanaticism of Pandulph. Meanwhile Hubert and the Bastard move from cynicism and detachment to self-possession and integrity.

At the beginning of the play, John is seen as a fallible, uncertain, imperfect monarch, successful at first, and with his moment of glory in the full Protestant tradition as he confronts Pandulph. He is, however, increasingly subject to the corrupting power of political need, so that his final collapse is total.

DRAMATIS PERSONÆ

1 KING JOHN
2 PRINCE HENRY, *son to the King*
3 ARTHUR, *Duke of Bretagne, nephew to the King*
4 EARL OF PEMBROKE
5 EARL OF ESSEX
6 EARL OF SALISBURY
7 LORD BIGOT
8 HUBERT DE BURGH
9 ROBERT FAULCONBRIDGE, *son to Sir Robert Faulconbridge*
10 PHILIP THE BASTARD, *his half-brother, later dubbed Richard Plantagenet*
11 JAMES GURNEY, *servant to Lady Faulconbridge*
12 PETER OF POMFRET, *a prophet*
13 EXECUTIONER
14 TWO MESSENGERS
15 ENGLISH HERALD
16 PHILIP, *King of France*
17 LEWIS, *the Dauphin*
18 LYMOGES, DUKE OF AUSTRIA
19 CARDINAL PANDULPH, *the Pope's legate*
20 MELUM, *a French Lord*
21 CHATILLON, *ambassador from France to King John*
22 CITIZEN *of Angiers*
23 FRENCH HERALD
24 QUEEN ELINOR, *mother to King John*
25 CONSTANCE, *mother of Arthur*
26 BLANCH *of Spain, niece to King John*
27 LADY FAULCONBRIDGE
28 NON-SPEAKING: *Lords, Citizens of Angiers, Sheriff, Officers, Soldiers and other Attendants*

14 THE MERCHANT OF VENICE

To try to win the hand of Portia, Bassanio borrows money from his friend, Antonio, who has to borrow that money from Shylock, a Jewish money-lender, on the agreement that if it is not repaid within three months, Shylock removes a pound in weight from Antonio's flesh.

Shylock's daughter, Jessica, elopes with Lorenzo, a gentile. Bassanio marries Portia.

Antonio's ships go aground, which means he cannot repay his loan. Shylock demands his bond. Disguised as a young lawyer and clerk, Portia and Nerissa, her maid, win Antonio's case in court. Shylock loses all and, on Antonio's insistence, becomes a Christian. After all, Antonio's ships are saved.

DRAMATIS PERSONÆ

1 THE DUKE OF VENICE
2 PRINCE OF MOROCCO *suitors to*
3 PRINCE OF ARRAGON *Portia*
4 ANTONIO, *a merchant of Venice*
5 BASSANIO, *his friend, suitor likewise to Portia*
6 SALANIO
7 SALARINO *friends to Antonio*
8 GRATIANO *and Bassanio*
9 SALERIO
10 LORENZO, *in love with Jessica*
11 SHYLOCK, *a rich Jew*
12 TUBAL, *a Jew, his friend*
13 LAUNCELOT GOBBO, *the clown servant to Shylock*
14 OLD GOBBO, *father to Launcelot*
15 LEONARDO, *servant to Bassanio*
16 BALTHASAR *servants to Portia*
17 STEPHANO
18 SERVANT *to Antonio*
19 SERVANT *to Portia*
20 PORTIA, *a rich heiress*
21 NERISSA, *her waiting-maid*
22 JESSICA, *daughter to Shylock*
23 NON-SPEAKING: *Magnificoes of Venice, Officers of the Court of Justice, Gaoler, Musicians, Servants to Portia, and other Attendants*

15 The First Part of
KING HENRY THE FOURTH

The Earl of Worcester, Earl of Northumberland and his son, Hotspur, plan a rebellion against Henry IV.

Prince Hal spends a lot of time in the tavern drinking with Falstaff and others, who hold up some rich travellers. For fun, the Prince robs Falstaff of the booty.

The Prince and Falstaff fight with the King at the Battle of Shrewsbury. The Prince is wounded but defends his father. Hotspur and the Prince duel and Hotspur is killed next to Falstaff, who is feigning death. Falstaff rises to stab the already-dead Hotspur, then demands a reward.

They end preparing for the next battle, as there are still more conspirators at arms.

DRAMATIS PERSONÆ

1 KING HENRY THE FOURTH
2 HENRY, PRINCE OF WALES } *sons to the King*
3 JOHN OF LANCASTER } *sons to the King*
4 EARL OF WESTMORELAND
5 SIR WALTER BLUNT
6 THOMAS PERCY, EARL OF WORCESTER
7 HENRY PERCY, EARL OF NORTHUMBERLAND
8 HENRY PERCY, *surnamed* HOTSPUR, *his son*
9 EDMUND MORTIMER, EARL OF MARCH
10 RICHARD SCROOP, ARCHBISHOP OF YORK
11 ARCHIBALD, EARL OF DOUGLAS
12 OWEN GLENDOWER
13 SIR RICHARD VERNON
14 SIR JOHN FALSTAFF
15 SIR MICHAEL, *a friend to the Archbishop of York*
16 POINS
17 GADSHILL
18 PETO
19 BARDOLPH
20 TWO CARRIERS
21 OSTLER
22 A CHAMBERLAIN
23 SEVERAL TRAVELLERS
24 A VINTNER
25 FRANCIS, *the drawer*
26 SHERIFF
27 TWO MESSENGERS
28 SERVANT *to Hotspur*
29 LADY PERCY, *wife to Hotspur, and sister to Mortimer*
30 LADY MORTIMER, *daughter to Glendower, and wife to Mortimer*
31 MISTRESS QUICKLY, *hostess of a tavern in Eastcheap*
32 NON-SPEAKING: *Lords, Officers, Drawers, Travellers and Attendants*

16 The Second Part of
KING HENRY THE FOURTH

The Archbishop of York and the Earl of Northumberland are conspiring against the King. The Archbishop is defeated by Prince John of Lancaster and the Earl of Northumberland by the Sheriff of Yorkshire.

Just before the King dies, he is reconciled with his son, Prince Henry. Henry changes from a riotous young prince to a just and good ruler. His old friend Falstaff still gets into mischief but is no longer suitable company for the new King, who sends him to prison, but promises him a small pension.

DRAMATIS PERSONÆ

1 KING HENRY THE FOURTH
2 HENRY, PRINCE OF WALES *afterwards* KING HENRY V
3 THOMAS, DUKE OF CLARENCE *his sons*
4 PRINCE JOHN OF LANCASTER
5 PRINCE HUMPHREY OF GLOUCESTER
6 EARL OF WARWICK
7 EARL OF WESTMORELAND
8 GOWER
9 HARCOURT
10 LORD CHIEF JUSTICE *of the King's Bench*
11 A SERVANT *of the Chief Justice*
12 EARL OF NORTHUMBERLAND
13 SCROOP, ARCHBISHOP OF YORK
14 LORD MOWBRAY
15 LORD HASTINGS
16 LORD BARDOLPH
17 SIR JOHN COLEVILLE
18 TRAVERS *retainers of*
19 MORTON *Northumberland*
20 SIR JOHN FALSTAFF
21 PAGE *to Falstaff*
22 BARDOLPH
23 PISTOL
24 POINS
25 PETO
26 SHALLOW *country justices*
27 SILENCE
28 DAVY, *servant to Shallow*
29 MOULDY
30 SHADOW
31 WART *recruits*
32 FEEBLE
33 BULLCALF
34 FANG *sheriff's officers*
35 SNARE
36 A PORTER
37 TWO DRAWERS
38 A MESSENGER
39 A BEADLE
40 TWO GROOMS
41 RUMOURS, *the Presenter*
42 A DANCER, *speaker of the Epilogue*
43 LADY NORTHUMBERLAND
44 LADY PERCY
45 MISTRESS QUICKLY, *hostess of a tavern in Eastcheap*
46 DOLL TEARSHEET
47 NON-SPEAKING: *Earl of Surrey, Blunt, Lords, Beadles, Musicians, and Attendants*
48 SCENE: *England*

17 MUCH ADO ABOUT NOTHING

Don Pedro, Prince of Aragon and two friends, Claudio and Benedick, stay in Messina with Leonato, the Governor. Don Pedro agrees to woo Leonato's daughter, Hero, on Claudio's behalf. Don Pedro, Leonato and Claudio plot to bring Beatrice, Leonato's niece, and Benedick together.

Hero is alleged to be unfaithful and Claudio denounces her, but the conspirators who planned this are discovered. For distrusting Hero, Benedick and Leonato both challenge Claudio to a duel but Claudio repents. All ends well and there is a double wedding: Claudio and Hero, Beatrice and Benedick.

DRAMATIS PERSONÆ

1 DON PEDRO, *Prince of Aragon*
2 DON JOHN, *his bastard brother*
3 CLAUDIO, *a young lord of Florence*
4 BENEDICK, *a young lord of Padua*
5 LEONATO, *Governor of Messina*
6 ANTONIO, *his brother*
7 BALTHASAR, *attendant on Don Pedro*
8 CONRADE *followers of*
9 BORACHIO *Don John*
10 FRIAR FRANCIS
11 DOGBERRY, *a constable*
12 VERGES, *a headborough*
13 A SEXTON
14 A BOY
15 TWO MESSENGERS
16 TWO WATCHMEN
17 A LORD
18 HERO, *daughter to Leonato*
19 BEATRICE, *niece to Leonato*
20 MARGARET *gentlewoman*
21 URSULA *attending on Hero*
22 NON-SPEAKING: *Messengers, Watch, Attendants, and Musicians*

18 The Life of KING HENRY THE FIFTH

The Archbishop of Canterbury advises the King that his descent from Isabella, the French Queen of Edward II, gives him the right to the French throne, and the Church would subsidise his going to war with France.

The Dauphin mockingly sends Henry a box of tennis-balls in response to his claims to certain French dukedoms, so Henry promises war. The English take Harfleur but the army is weakened by disease and the French are much stronger. Henry encourages his soldiers and against all odds the French are defeated, and Henry takes the French throne.

DRAMATIS PERSONÆ

1 KING HENRY THE FIFTH
2 DUKE OF GLOUCESTER *brothers to the King*
3 DUKE OF BEDFORD
4 DUKE OF EXETER, *uncle to the King*
5 DUKE OF YORK, *cousin to the King*
6 EARL OF SALISBURY
7 EARL OF WESTMORELAND
8 EARL OF WARWICK
9 ARCHBISHOP OF CANTERBURY
10 BISHOP OF ELY
11 EARL OF CAMBRIDGE
12 LORD SCROOP
13 SIR THOMAS GREY
14 SIR THOMAS ERPINGHAM *officers in King Henry's army*
15 GOWER
16 FLUELLEN
17 MACMORRIS
18 JAMY
19 BATES *soldiers in King Henry's army*
20 COURT
21 WILLIAMS
22 PISTOL
23 NYM
24 BARDOLPH
25 BOY
26 A HERALD
27 THREE MESSENGERS
28 CHARLES THE SIXTH, *King of France*
29 LEWIS, THE DAUPHIN
30 DUKE OF BURGUNDY
31 DUKE OF ORLEANS
32 DUKE OF BOURBON
33 THE CONSTABLE OF FRANCE
34 RAMBURES *French Lords*
35 GRANDPRÉ
36 GOVERNOR OF HARFLEUR
37 MONTJOY, *a French Herald*
38 AMBASSADOR *to the King of England*
39 FRENCH PRISONER
40 ISABEL, *Queen of France*
41 KATHERINE, *daughter to Charles and Isabel*
42 ALICE, *a lady attending on her*
43 HOSTESS *of a tavern in Eastcheap, formerly* MISTRESS QUICKLY, *and now married to Pistol*
44 CHORUS
45 NON-SPEAKING: *Lords, Ladies, Officers, Soldiers, Citizens, and Attendants*

19 JULIUS CÆSAR

Cassius and other conspirators plot to kill Julius Caesar and to make Brutus their leader. The group stab Caesar on the Ides of March, as had been prophesied. Antony is given permission to speak at Caesar's funeral and the crowd are enraged at what has happened and riot. Brutus and Cassius flee from Rome but raise armies. Brutus is visited by Caesar's ghost. Both Brutus and Cassius commit suicide when defeated in battle.

DRAMATIS PERSONÆ

1 JULIUS CÆSAR, *later as a* GHOST
2 OCTAVIUS CÆSAR
3 MARCUS ANTONIUS
4 M. ÆMILIUS LEPIDUS
Triumvirs after the death of Julius Cæsar
5 CICERO
6 PUBLIUS
7 POPILIUS LENA
Senators
8 MARCUS BRUTUS
9 CASSIUS
10 CASCA
11 TREBONIUS
12 LIGARIUS
13 DECIUS BRUTUS
14 METELLUS CIMBER
conspirators against Julius Cæsar
15 CINNA
16 FLAVIUS
17 MARULLUS
Tribunes
18 ARTEMIDORUS OF CNIDOS, *a teacher of rhetoric*
19 A SOOTHSAYER
20 CINNA, *a poet*
21 ANOTHER POET
22 LUCILIUS
23 TITINIUS
24 MESSALA
25 YOUNG CATO
friends to Brutus and Cassius
26 VOLUMNIUS
27 VARRO
28 CLITUS
29 CLAUDIUS
30 STRATO
servants to Brutus
31 LUCIUS
32 DARDANIUS
33 PINDARUS, *servant to Cassius*
34 TWO COMMONERS
35 A SERVANT *to Cæsar*
36 A SERVANT *to Antony*
37 A SERVANT *to Octavius*
38 FOUR CITIZENS
39 THREE SOLDIERS
40 A MESSENGER
41 CALPURNIA, *wife to Cæsar*
42 PORTIA, *wife to Brutus*
43 NON-SPEAKING: *Senators, Citizens, Guards, Soldiers, and Attendants*

Oliver has plotted that Charles will kill Oliver's brother, Orlando, in a wrestling match. Orlando wins. Rosalind, the daughter of the banished Duke Senior, and Orlando fall in love. Duke Frederick banishes Rosalind but Duke Frederick's daughter, Celia and Rosalind (disguised as a man) flee together with the court clown, Touchstone. Orlando and his old servant, Adam, also flee.

They arrive in the forest of Arden, where Duke Senior is living. Silvius and Phebe arrive but Phebe falls in love with the disguised Rosalind!

Orlando is wounded by a lioness, while saving Oliver, sent to arrest Orlando. Oliver and Celia fall in love and the play ends with four weddings.

DRAMATIS PERSONÆ

1 DUKE SENIOR, *living in banishment*
2 FREDERICK, *his brother, and usurper of his dominions*
3 AMIENS *lords attending on the*
4 JAQUES *banished Duke*
5 LE BEAU, *a courtier attending upon Frederick*
6 CHARLES, *wrestler to Frederick*
7 OLIVER
8 JAQUES *sons of Sir Rowland de Boys*
9 ORLANDO
10 ADAM *servants to Oliver*
11 DENNIS
12 TOUCHSTONE, *a clown*
13 SIR OLIVER MARTEXT, *a vicar*
14 CORIN *shepherds*
15 SILVIUS
16 WILLIAM, *a country fellow, in love with Audrey*
17 THREE LORDS, *attending on the banished Duke*
18 TWO LORDS, *attending on Frederick*
19 TWO PAGES, *attending on the banished Duke*
20 HYMEN
21 A FORESTER
22 ROSALIND, *daughter to the banished Duke*
23 CELIA, *daughter to Frederick*
24 PHEBE, *a shepherdess*
25 AUDREY, *a country wench*
26 NON-SPEAKING: *Lords, Foresters, and Attendants*

21 HAMLET
Prince of Denmark

Hamlet is told by the ghost of his father that he was murdered by his brother Claudius, now King. Hamlet feigns madness while plotting revenge. He organises a play depicting his father's death to confirm Claudius' guilt. While warning his mother, Hamlet kills Polonius, who is eavesdropping. Claudius sends Hamlet to England to be killed but he escapes to return.

Ophelia, Polonius' daughter, has drowned herself. The King proposes a duel between Hamlet and the son of Polonius, Laertes. Hamlet is wounded by a poisoned sword which he then takes to kill Laertes and the King. The Queen drinks poisoned wine prepared for Hamlet, and Hamlet dies from his wound.

DRAMATIS PERSONÆ

1 CLAUDIUS, *King of Denmark*
2 HAMLET, *son to the late, and nephew to the present, King*
3 POLONIUS, *Lord Chamberlain*
4 HORATIO, *friend to Hamlet*
5 LAERTES, *son to Polonius*
6 VOLTIMAND
7 CORNELIUS
8 ROSENCRANTZ *Courtiers*
9 GUILDENSTERN
10 OSRIC
11 A GENTLEMAN
12 A PRIEST
13 MARCELLUS *Officers*
14 BERNARDO
15 FRANCISCO, *a soldier*
16 REYNALDO, *servant to Polonius*
17 FIVE PLAYERS
18 TWO CLOWNS, *gravediggers*
19 FORTINBRAS, *Prince of Norway*
20 A CAPTAIN
21 ENGLISH AMBASSADORS
22 A LORD
23 A SOLDIER
24 TWO MESSENGERS
25 A SERVANT *to Horatio*
26 DANES
27 GHOST *of Hamlet's father*
28 GERTRUDE, *Queen of Denmark, and mother to Hamlet*
29 OPHELIA, *daughter to Polonius*
30 NON-SPEAKING: *Lords, Ladies, Officers, Soldiers, Sailors, and other Attendants*

22 THE MERRY WIVES OF WINDSOR

A story about life in the comfortable, self-assured community of Windsor where daughters Page and Ford, enterprising and independent women, were involved in the active pursuit of husband finding. The story involves all the representative characters of a community: two professional men, a doctor and a parson, the host of the inn and a born gossip.

The action of the play takes place during a holiday time, with the accent on sport and the townsfolk all participating. The professor instructs his student to court one of the wives. They use their powers of invention to administer lessons back to the professor who is threatening their way of life. There is much revenge in this play with many complicated intrigues.

DRAMATIS PERSONÆ

1 SIR JOHN FALSTAFF
2 FENTON, *a gentleman*
3 SHALLOW, *a country justice*
4 SLENDER, *cousin to Shallow*
5 FORD } *two gentlemen dwelling at*
6 PAGE } *Windsor*
7 WILLIAM PAGE, *a boy, son to Page*
8 SIR HUGH EVANS, *a Welsh parson*
9 DOCTOR CAIUS, *a French physician*
10 HOST *of the Garter Inn*
11 BARDOLPH }
12 PISTOL } *sharpers attending on Falstaff*
13 NYM }
14 ROBIN, *page to Falstaff*
15 SIMPLE, *servant to Slender*
16 JOHN RUGBY, *servant to Doctor Caius*
17 TWO SERVANTS *to Ford*
18 MISTRESS FORD
19 MISTRESS PAGE
20 ANNE PAGE, *her daughter*
21 MISTRESS QUICKLY, *servant to Doctor Caius*
22 SOME CHILDREN, *as fairies*
23 NON-SPEAKING: *Servants to Page and Ford*

23 TWELFTH NIGHT
Or, What You Will

Viola disguises herself as Cesario and becomes a page to Orsino, who is in love with Olivia. Orsino sends Cesario to woo Olivia on his behalf but Olivia falls in love with Cesario. Malvolio is led to believe that Olivia loves him: Olivia thinks he is mad.

Sir Toby Belch challenges Cesario to a duel, which is stopped by Antonio, who mistakes Cesario (Viola) for her brother, Sebastian, whom Viola thought was dead. Sebastian is mistaken for Cesario by Sir Toby and friends and a fight is broken up by Olivia, who also thinks Sebastian is Cesario. Eventually all is sorted out.

DRAMATIS PERSONÆ

1 ORSINO, DUKE OF ILLYRIA
2 SEBASTIAN, *brother to Viola*
3 ANTONIO, *a sea captain, friend to Sebastian*
4 A SEA CAPTAIN, *friend to Viola*
5 VALENTINE *gentlemen attending*
6 CURIO *on the Duke*
7 SIR TOBY BELCH, *uncle to Olivia*
8 SIR ANDREW AGUECHEEK
9 MALVOLIO, *steward to Olivia*
10 FABIAN *servants to*
11 FESTE, A CLOWN *Olivia*
12 TWO OFFICERS
13 A PRIEST
14 A SERVANT *to Olivia*
15 OLIVIA
16 VIOLA
17 MARIA, *Olivia's woman*
18 NON-SPEAKING: *Lords, Sailors, Officers, Musicians, and other Attendants*

24 TROILUS AND CRESSIDA

Achilles abandons the Greeks in their battle for Troy and Ajax is chosen as their new champion. In return for Helen, the Greeks will stop the siege but Paris, in love with Helen, will not give her up.

Troilus and Cressida swear eternal love to each other but her father, Calchas, a deserter of Troy, requests that she is exchanged for the Greek prisoner, Antenor. Cressida decides it better to shift her allegiance and Diomed claims his right to Cressida and disillusioned, Troilus promises revenge. Hector and Troilus go into battle and Achilles is angered into fighting. Hector spares Achilles' life but then Achilles plots the murder of Hector. The fall of Troy follows.

DRAMATIS PERSONÆ

1 PRIAM, *King of Troy*
2 HECTOR
3 TROILUS
4 PARIS *his sons*
5 DEIPHOBUS
6 HELENUS
7 MARGARELON, *a bastard son of Priam*
8 ÆNEAS *Trojan commanders*
9 ANTENOR
10 CALCHAS, *a Trojan priest, taking part with the Greeks*
11 PANDARUS, *uncle to Cressida*
12 AGAMEMNON, *the Grecian general*
13 MENELAUS, *his brother*
14 ACHILLES
15 AJAX
16 ULYSSES *Grecian*
17 NESTOR *commanders*
18 DIOMEDES
19 PATROCLUS
20 THERSITES, *a deformed and scurrilous Grecian*
21 ALEXANDER, *servant to Cressida*
22 A BOY, *servant to Troilus*
23 A SERVANT *to Paris*
24 A SERVANT *to Diomedes*
25 A MYRMIDON
26 HELEN, *wife to Menelaus*
27 ANDROMACHE, *wife to Hector*
28 CASSANDRA, *daughter to Priam, a prophetess*
29 CRESSIDA, *daughter to Calchas*
30 NON-SPEAKING: *Trojan and Greek Soldiers, Myrmidons, and Attendants*

25 ALL'S WELL THAT ENDS WELL

This work is mature, subtle and haunting; it is thought of as a 'dark comedy' or 'problem play'. It is full of issues that can tax and vex the mind. It is a love story, although not full of happiness. It does, however, end as well as it can. Helena is rejected by Bertram on the grounds of her inferior class, while the King speaks rationally and passionately about the value of merit over birth.

The scene begins with Helena beginning her 'cure'. This is a 'bed trick' where she must trick her husband into making love to her without him knowing it is her. This she does, but although she becomes pregnant, he loves the 'shadow' of her and there is no firm close or direction. It is a play about holding on to the 'Yetness' of things, when they are out of sight but real.

DRAMATIS PERSONÆ

1 KING OF FRANCE
2 DUKE OF FLORENCE
3 BERTRAM, *Count of Rousillon*
4 LAFEU, *an old lord*
5 PAROLLES, *a follower of Bertram*
6 TWO FRENCH LORDS *in the Florentine service*
7 RINALDO, *steward to the Countess*
8 A CLOWN, *servant to the Countess*
9 THREE FRENCH LORDS, *attending on the King*
10 A GENTLEMAN, *a stranger*
11 TWO SOLDIERS
12 A MESSENGER
13 COUNTESS OF ROUSILLON, *mother to Bertram*
14 HELENA, *a gentlewoman protected by the Countess*
15 A WIDOW *of Florence*
16 DIANA, *daughter to the Widow*
17 MARIANA, *neighbour and friend to the Widow*
18 NON-SPEAKING: *Lords, Officers; Soldiers, French and Florentine; Violetta, neighbour and friend to the Widow; Attendants*

26 MEASURE FOR MEASURE

Duke Vincentio leaves Angelo in charge of Vienna, but disguises himself as a friar to keep an eye on things. Angelo starts a clean-up campaign. Claudio receives the death penalty for fornication. Isabella, about to enter a nunnery, pleads for his mercy, Angelo falls in love with her and offers to spare Claudio if she will give herself to him. At the 'friar's' suggestion, Isabella pretends to accept Angelo's proposal, but Mariana takes her place.

Angelo does not keep his promise and orders Claudio's execution. A pirate is substituted for Claudio, the returned Duke condemns Angelo to death but Mariana begs for his life. The Duke pardons Claudio and Angelo, and asks Isabella to marry him.

DRAMATIS PERSONÆ

1 VINCENTIO, *the Duke*
2 ANGELO, *the Deputy*
3 ESCALUS, *an ancient Lord*
4 CLAUDIO, *a young gentleman*
5 LUCIO, *a fantastic*
6 TWO GENTLEMEN
7 PROVOST
8 THOMAS } *two friars*
9 PETER }
10 A JUSTICE
11 VARRIUS
12 ELBOW, *a simple constable*
13 FROTH, *a foolish gentleman*
14 POMPEY, *servant to Mistress Overdone*
15 ABHORSON, *an executioner*
16 BARNARDINE, *a dissolute prisoner*
17 A BOY
18 A MESSENGER
19 A SERVANT *to Angelo*
20 ISABELLA, *sister to Claudio*
21 MARIANA, *betrothed to Angelo*
22 JULIET, *beloved of Claudio*
23 FRANCISCA, *a nun*
24 MISTRESS OVERDONE, *a bawd*
25 NON-SPEAKING: *Lords, Officers, Citizens, and Attendants*

27 OTHELLO, the Moor of Venice

Othello is defending Cyprus againt the Turks. He is secretly married to Desdemona. Iago and Roderigo, in love with Desdemona, plot against Othello and his lieutenant, Cassio, by making Othello suspect Desdemona and Cassio of adultery. Othello kills Desdemona. Iago's wife, Emilia, reveals the plot to Othello but is then killed by her husband. Iago is captured and Othello kills himself.

DRAMATIS PERSONÆ

1 DUKE OF VENICE
2 BRABANTIO, *a Senator*
3 TWO SENATORS
4 GRATIANO, *brother of Brabantio*
5 LODOVICO, *kinsman to Brabantio*
6 OTHELLO, *a noble Moor in the service of the Venetian state*
7 CASSIO, *his lieutenant*
8 IAGO, *his ancient*
9 RODERIGO, *a Venitian gentleman*
10 MONTANO, *Othello's predecessor in the government of Cyprus*
11 CLOWN, *servant to Othello*
12 TWO GENTLEMEN, *of Venice*
13 FOUR GENTLEMEN, *of Cyprus*
14 AN OFFICER
15 A HERALD
16 A MESSENGER
17 A SAILOR
18 A MUSICIAN
19 DESDEMONA, *daughter to Brabantio and wife to Othello*
20 EMILIA, *wife to Iago*
21 BIANCA, *mistress to Cassio*
22 NON-SPEAKING: *Officers, Gentlemen, Musicians, and Attendants*

28 KING LEAR

King Lear hands his kingdom over to two of his daughters, Goneril and Regan, and shares his time between them, but each plots for dominance. His other daughter, Cordelia, is married to the King of France without a dowry and cut out of Lear's will. The very old King Lear goes mad and Cordelia brings an army from France to rescue him, but Cordelia is murdered in prison and Lear dies.

Meanwhile, the Earl of Gloucester is tricked by his bastard son, Edmund, into believing his legitimate son, Edgar, is a traitor, although Edmund is plotting to dispose of his father and brother. Edgar saves Gloucester and kills Edmund.

DRAMATIS PERSONÆ

1 LEAR, *King of Britain*
2 KING OF FRANCE
3 DUKE OF BURGUNDY
4 DUKE OF CORNWALL
5 DUKE OF ALBANY
6 EARL OF KENT
7 EARL OF GLOUCESTER
8 EDGAR, *son to Gloucester*
9 EDMUND, *bastard son to Gloucester*
10 CURAN, *a courtier*
11 OLD MAN, *tenant to Gloucester*
12 A DOCTOR
13 FOOL
14 OSWALD, *steward to Goneril*
15 TWO CAPTAINS
16 A GENTLEMAN, *attendant on Cordelia*
17 A GENTLEMAN, *attendant on Lear*
18 A KNIGHT, *attendant on Lear*
19 A HERALD
20 THREE SERVANTS *to Cornwall*
21 TWO MESSENGERS
22 GONERIL
23 REGAN *daughters to Lear*
24 CORDELIA
25 NON-SPEAKING: *Knights of Lear's train, Captains, Soldiers, and Attendants*

29 MACBETH

Three witches prophesy Macbeth will be King and Banquo will be father to a line of kings. Lady Macbeth urges her husband to murder the King. Macbeth is crowned and to stop the witches prophecy, he hires murderers to kill Banquo and his son Fleance, but Fleance escapes. Macbeth sees the ghost of Banquo and he seeks out the witches who tell him to beware of Macduff, and repeat that descendants of Banquo will become kings.

Macbeth has Macduff's wife and children murdered; Macduff and his men beseige Macbeth's castle. Lady Macbeth commits suicide, Macduff kills Macbeth, and Malcolm, the eldest son of Duncan, becomes King.

DRAMATIS PERSONÆ

1 DUNCAN, *King of Scotland*
2 MALCOLM *his son*
3 DONALBAIN
4 MACBETH *generals of the*
5 BANQUO *King's army*
6 MACDUFF
7 LENNOX
8 ROSS *noblemen of*
9 MENTEITH *Scotland*
10 ANGUS
11 CAITHNESS
12 FLEANCE, *son to Banquo*
13 SIWARD, *Earl of Northumberland, general of the English forces*
14 YOUNG SIWARD, *his son*
15 SEYTON, *an officer attending on Macbeth*
16 BOY, *son of Macduff*
17 AN ENGLISH DOCTOR
18 A SCOTCH DOCTOR
19 A LORD
20 A PORTER
21 AN OLD MAN
22 A SERGEANT
23 TWO MESSENGERS
24 AN ATTENDANT *on Macbeth*
25 A SERVANT *to Lady Macbeth*
26 THREE MURDERERS
27 LADY MACBETH
28 LADY MACDUFF
29 A GENTLEWOMAN, *attending on Lady Macbeth*
30 HECATE
31 THREE WITCHES
32 THREE APPARITIONS
33 NON-SPEAKING: *Lords, Ladies, Officers, Soldiers, Ghosts, and Attendants*

30 ANTONY AND CLEOPATRA

Antony has neglected his duties in the Roman Empire to pursue a love affair with Cleopatra in Egypt, and has to return home. To please Caesar, Antony agrees to marry Octavia, Caesar's sister. Caesar kills Lepidus, who has been used to defeat Pompey.

Caesar and Antony control the Empire. Antony returns to Cleopatra, which causes Caesar to fight with him. Cleopatra helps Antony but he is defeated in battle. He commits suicide hearing a false report that Cleopatra is dead. Cleopatra commits suicide and they are buried together.

DRAMATIS PERSONÆ

1 MARK ANTONY
2 OCTAVIUS CÆSAR *triumvirs*
3 M. ÆMILIUS LEPIDUS
4 SEXTUS POMPEIUS
5 DOMITIUS ENOBARBUS
6 VENTIDIUS
7 EROS *friends to*
8 SCARUS *Antony*
9 DERCETAS
10 DEMETRIUS
11 PHILO
12 MECÆNAS
13 AGRIPPA
14 DOLABELLA
15 PROCULEIUS *friends to Cæsar*
16 THYREUS
17 GALLUS
18 MENAS
19 MENECRATES *friends to Pompey*
20 VARRIUS
21 TAURUS, *lieutenant-general to Cæsar*
22 CANIDIUS, *lieutenant-general to Antony*
23 SILIUS, *an officer in Ventidius' army*
24 EUPHRONIUS, *an ambassador from Antony to Cæsar*
25 ALEXAS
26 MARDIAN, *a eunuch, attendants*
27 SELEUCUS *on Cleopatra*
28 DIOMEDES
29 A SOOTHSAYER
30 A CLOWN
31 FIVE MESSENGERS
32 AN EGYPTIAN
33 TWO SERVANTS *to Pompey*
34 A CAPTAIN *of Antony's army*
35 FOUR SOLDIERS *of Antony's army*
36 FOUR SOLDIERS *of Caesar's army*
37 TWO GUARDS *to Cleopatra*
38 THREE GUARDS *of Antony's army*
39 TWO ATTENDANTS *on Antony*
40 ONE ATTENDANT *on Cleopatra*
41 CLEOPATRA, *Queen of Egypt*
42 OCTAVIA, *sister to Cæsar and wife to Antony*
43 CHARMIAN *attendants on*
44 IRAS *Cleopatra*
45 NON-SPEAKING: *Officers, Soldiers, Guards, Servitors, and Attendants*

31 CORIOLANUS

Coriolanus, a great warrior, stands for election as consul but fails because he disagrees with certain policies and he is declared a traitor. In revenge, he leads the Volsces, the enemy forces, against Rome. The Romans beg Coriolanus to spare the city but it is only his mother, Volumnia, who persuades him. Coriolanus is assassinated for betraying the Volsces.

DRAMATIS PERSONÆ

1 CAIUS MARCIUS, *afterwards* CAIUS MARCIUS CORIOLANUS
2 TITUS LARTIUS } *generals against the Volscians*
3 COMINIUS }
4 MENENIUS AGRIPPA, *friend to Coriolanus*
5 SICINIUS VELUTUS } *tribunes of the people*
6 JUNIUS BRUTUS }
7 YOUNG MARCIUS, *son to Coriolanus*
8 A ROMAN HERALD
9 NICANOR, *a Roman*
10 AN ÆDILE
11 TWO PATRICIANS
12 TWO OFFICERS
13 A LIEUTENANT *to Lartius*
14 TWO SENATORS
15 SEVEN CITIZENS
16 THREE MESSENGERS
17 THREE SOLDIERS
18 TULLUS AUFIDIUS, *general of the Volscians*
19 A LIEUTENANT *to Aufidius*
20 THREE CONSPIRATORS *with Aufidius*
21 A CITIZEN *of Antium*
22 TWO LORDS
23 TWO SENTRIES
24 TWO SENATORS
25 THREE SOLDIERS
26 ADRIAN, *A Volscian*
27 THREE SERVANTS *to Aufidius*
28 VOLUMNIA, *mother to Coriolanus*
29 VIRGILIA, *wife to Coriolanus*
30 VALERIA, *friend to Virgilia*
31 GENTLEWOMAN, *attending on Virgilia*
32 NON-SPEAKING: *Roman and Volscian Senators, Patricians, Soldiers, Citizens, Lictors, and Attendants*

32 TIMON OF ATHENS

This is the bitterest and most negative of Shakespeare's tragedies. The story begins with an obviously wealthy Timon – however he has no family, or close friends, and no reference to his past. He is a philanthropist, giving lavishly to those he considers his friends. Suddenly creditors demand repayment and he is bankrupt.

Timon sees this as a lovely opportunity for his friends to prove their brotherhood and his conviction in the goodness of man. Each friend turns him down. The shock gives a cynical betrayal of his trust in human nature and he transforms his love of humanity to hatred, the philanthropist becomes misanthropist. He summons his 'friends' to a last feast and serves them warm water, delivers a scathing speech and drives them out with blows. Then he retires to the woods to live on roots and berries. Eventually when his desire to curse mankind is exhausted he makes a tomb by the sea, and dies.

DRAMATIS PERSONÆ

1 TIMON *of Athens*
2 LUCIUS
3 LUCULLUS *flattering lords*
4 SEMPRONIUS
5 VENTIDIUS, *one of Timon's false friends*
6 ALCIBIADES, *an Athenian captain*
7 APEMANTUS, *a churlish philosopher*
8 FLAVIUS, *steward to Timon*
9 A POET
10 A PAINTER
11 A JEWELLER
12 A MERCHANT
13 AN OLD ATHENIAN
14 A PAGE
15 A FOOL
16 THREE STRANGERS
17 A SOLDIER
18 THREE BANDITTI
19 FOUR SENATORS
20 FOUR LORDS
21 THREE MESSENGERS
22 FLAMINIUS
23 LUCILIUS *Servants to Timon*
24 SERVILIUS
25 CAPHIS
26 PHILOTUS *Servants to*
27 TITUS *Timon's creditors*
28 HORTENSIUS
29 THREE SERVANTS *to Timon*
30 TWO SERVANTS *to Varro*
31 A SERVANT *to Isidore*
32 A SERVANT *to Lucullus*
33 A SERVANT *to Lucius*
34 PHRYNIA *mistresses to*
35 TIMANDRA *Alcibiades*
36 CUPID
37 AMAZONS *in the mask*
38 NON-SPEAKING: *Lords, Senators, Officers, Soldiers, Banditti, and Attendants*

33 PERICLES
Prince of Tyre

This play is based upon the ancient tale of Apollonius of Tyre, a Greek romance. It is a profoundly moral work, although it may seem too one sided. Pericles is an ardent young man seeking a bride in the first scene and by the end of the play a father in mid-life. He has undergone much experience and suffering during these fifteen years.

Twice the sea wrecks Pericles. The sea threatens and comforts; destroys and rebuilds; separates and unites. During this time Pericles loses his wife and then, as she grows to womanhood, his daughter. He continues to live, but is dead to the world.

DRAMATIS PERSONÆ

1 GOWER, *as chorus*
2 ANTIOCHUS, *King of Antioch*
3 PERICLES, *Prince of Tyre*
4 HELICANUS } *two lords of Tyre*
5 ESCANES }
6 SIMONIDES, *King of Pentapolis*
7 CLEON, *governor of Tarsus*
8 LYSIMACHUS, *governor of Mytilene*
9 CERIMON, *a lord of Ephesus*
10 THALIARD, *a lord of Antioch*
11 PHILEMON, *servant to Cerimon*
12 LEONINE, *servant to Dionyza*
13 MARSHAL
14 A PANDAR
15 BOULT, *his servant*
16 A MESSENGER
17 THREE LORDS *of Tyre*
18 A LORD *of Tarsus*
19 THREE FISHERMEN
20 A KNIGHT, *attending on Simonides*
21 TWO SAILORS *of Pentapolis*
22 A SERVANT *of Cerimon*
23 THREE PIRATES
24 TWO GENTLEMEN *of Mytilene*
25 A SAILOR *of Tyre*
26 A SAILOR *of Mytilene*
27 FIVE KNIGHTS, *suitors to Thaisa*
28 THE DAUGHTER *of Antiochus*
29 DIONYZA, *wife to Cleon*
30 THAISA, *daughter to Simonides*
31 MARINA, *daughter to Pericles and Thaisa*
32 LYCHORIDA, *nurse to Marina*
33 A BAWD
34 DIANA
35 NON-SPEAKING: *Lords, Knights, Gentlemen, Sailors, and Attendants*

34 CYMBELINE

Cymbeline opposes Imogen's marriage to Posthumus, who is banished to Italy. The Queen plots to take control of the country from Cymbeline and make Cloten, her son, king with Imogen as his bride, and she causes the Romans to declare war on Britain. When Posthumus believes Imogen has been unfaithful, he orders her killed, but she is not.

Belarius has lived for years in a cave after kidnapping Guiderius and Arviragus, sons of Cymbeline. Cloten is killed by Guiderius. The Romans are defeated and peace is restored. Posthumus repents, he and Imogen are reunited, the Queen dies, and the King is reunited with his sons.

DRAMATIS PERSONÆ

1 CYMBELINE, *King of Britain*
2 CLOTEN, *son to the Queen by a former husband*
3 POSTHUMUS LEONATUS, *a gentleman, husband to Imogen*
4 BELARIUS, *a banished lord disguised under the name of Morgan*
5 GUIDERIUS
6 ARVIRAGUS
sons to Cymbeline, disguised under the names of Polydore and Cadwal, supposed sons to Morgan
7 PHILARIO, *friend to Posthumus*
8 IACHIMO, *friend to Philario*
Italians
9 CAIUS LUCIUS, *general of the Roman forces*
10 PISANIO, *servant to Posthumus*
11 CORNELIUS, *a physician*
12 A ROMAN CAPTAIN
13 TWO BRITISH CAPTAINS
14 A FRENCHMAN
15 A SPANIARD
16 A DUTCHMAN
friends to Philario
17 TWO LORDS *of Cymbeline's court*
18 TWO GENTLEMEN *of Cymbeline's court*
19 TWO GAOLERS
20 A SOOTHSAYER
21 A TRIBUNE
22 TWO SENATORS
23 AN ATTENDANT *on Cymbeline*
24 TWO MESSENGERS
25 QUEEN, *wife to Cymbeline*
26 IMOGEN, *daughter to Cymbeline by a former Queen*
27 HELEN, *a lady attending on Imogen*
28 A LADY *attending on the Queen*
29 SICILIUS LEONATUS, *father to Posthumus*
30 TWO LEONATI, *brothers to Posthumus*
31 MOTHER *to Posthumus*
Apparitions
32 JUPITER
33 NON-SPEAKING: *Lords, Ladies, Roman Senators and Tribunes, Musicians, Officers, Captains, Soldiers, and Attendants*

35 THE WINTER'S TALE

Leontes, King of Sicilia, thinks Hermione, his wife, and his friend, Polixenes, King of Bohemia, are having an affair. Leontes asks Camillo to murder Polixenes but instead he flees the country with Polixenes, increasing Leontes' suspicions. Leontes imprisons Hermione and orders their newborn daughter to be abandoned.

The Oracle in Delphi proclaims Hermione not guilty. Their son, Mamillius, and then Hermione die. The abandoned daughter, Perdita, is found by a shepherd and when sixteen is courted by Florizel, Polixenes son. Polixenes denounces his son and threatens Perdita and the shepherd. When her identity is discovered, the kings and their children are reconciled and Perdita and Florizel are married.

DRAMATIS PERSONÆ

1 TIME *as Chorus*
2 LEONTES, *King of Sicilia*
3 MAMILLIUS, *young Prince of Sicilia*
4 CAMILLO
5 ANTIGONUS
6 CLEOMENES
7 DION
four Lords of Sicilia
8 POLIXENES, *King of Bohemia*
9 FLORIZEL, *Prince of Bohemia*
10 ARCHIDAMUS, *a Lord of Bohemia*
11 OLD SHEPHERD, *reputed father of Perdita*
12 CLOWN, *his son*
13 AUTOLYCUS, *a rogue*
14 A MARINER
15 A GAOLER
16 THREE GENTLEMEN
17 A LORD, *attending on Leontes*
18 THREE SERVANTS *to Leontes*
19 AN OFFICER
20 A SERVANT *to the Old Shepherd*
21 HERMIONE, *Queen to Leontes*
22 PERDITA, *daughter to Leontes and Hermione*
23 PAULINA, *wife to Antigonus*
24 EMILIA, *a lady attending on Hermione*
25 MOPSA
26 DORCAS
shepherdesses
27 TWO LADIES *attending on Hermione*
28 NON-SPEAKING: *Lords, Ladies, Gentlemen, Officers, Servants, Shepherds, Shepherdesses, and Attendants*

36 THE TEMPEST

Prospero lost his dukedom through a conspiracy between his brother, Antonio, and King Alonso. He was abandoned with his daughter, Miranda, at sea and arrived on an island. Prospero using magic powers, releases a spirit, Ariel, who controls a storm during which Alonso and his fellow shipmates are shipwrecked. Ariel lures the King's son, Ferdinand, to Prospero. Ferdinand falls in love with Miranda.

When Ferdinand is found with Prospero, Alonso begs pardon for the wrongs done to Prospero and he gives him back his dukedom. They are all able to return in the ship to Italy.

DRAMATIS PERSONÆ

1 ALONSO, *King of Naples*
2 SEBASTIAN, *his brother*
3 PROSPERO, *the right Duke of Milan*
4 ANTONIO, *his brother, the usurping Duke of Milan*
5 FERDINAND, *son to the King of Naples*
6 GONZALO, *an honest old counsellor*
7 ADRIAN
8 FRANCISCO *Lords*
9 CALIBAN, *a savage and deformed slave*
10 TRINCULO, *a jester*
11 STEPHANO, *a drunken butler*
12 MASTER *of a ship*
13 BOATSWAIN
14 MARINERS
15 MIRANDA, *daughter to Prospero*
16 ARIEL, *an airy spirit*
17 IRIS
18 CERES *Spirits*
19 JUNO
20 NON-SPEAKING: *Nymphs and Reapers, presented by Spirits; and other Spirits attending on Prospero*

37 The famous History of the Life of KING HENRY THE EIGHTH

This is Shakespeare's only play to be entitled a 'Famous History' and takes unusual care to be historically authentic. The play's form is wave-like, with great swells of events bearing the King and leading figures upward and downward to and from high places.

The Duke of Buckingham, having decided to challenge the over-wearing Wolsey, is arrested before he can take measures either of attack or defence. Queen Katharine makes clear her courage by speaking for him and against Cardinal Wolsey; Buckingham is executed. Meanwhile the King starts to raise Anne Boleyn (Bullen) to the throne, as Katharine falls from grace and there is a great divorce trial. Then even Wolsey is convicted of exorbitant gains and falls from power. To counter-balance this, Anne is crowned and Princess Elizabeth is born. Henry VIII finishes in a triumph and is clearly meant to celebrate the reign.

DRAMATIS PERSONÆ

1 KING HENRY THE EIGHTH
2 CARDINAL WOLSEY
3 CARDINAL CAMPEIUS
4 CAPUCIUS, *ambassador from the Emperor Charles V*
5 CRANMER, *Archbishop of Canterbury*
6 DUKE OF NORFOLK
7 DUKE OF BUCKINGHAM
8 DUKE OF SUFFOLK
9 EARL OF SURREY
10 LORD CHAMBERLAIN
11 LORD CHANCELLOR
12 GARDINER, *Bishop of Winchester*
13 BISHOP OF LINCOLN
14 LORD ABERGAVENNY
15 LORD SANDS
16 SIR HENRY GUILDFORD
17 SIR THOMAS LOVELL
18 SIR ANTHONY DENNY
19 SIR NICHOLAS VAUX
20 TWO SECRETARIES *to Wolsey*
21 CROMWELL, *servant to Wolsey*
22 GRIFFITH, *gentleman-usher to Queen Katharine*
23 THREE GENTLEMEN
24 DOCTOR BUTTS, *physician to the King*
25 GARTER KING-AT-ARMS
26 SURVEYOR *to the Duke of Buckingham*
27 BRANDON
28 SERGEANT-AT-ARMS
29 DOOR-KEEPER *of the Council-chamber*
30 PORTER
31 MAN, *to the Porter*
32 PAGE *to Gardiner*
33 A CRIER
34 A MESSENGER
35 A SCRIBE
36 A SERVANT *to Wolsey*
37 QUEEN KATHARINE, *wife to King Henry, afterwards divorced*
38 ANNE BULLEN, *her Maid of Honour, afterwards Queen*
39 AN OLD LADY, *friend to Anne Bullen*
40 PATIENCE, *woman to Queen Katharine*
41 NON-SPEAKING: *Lords and Ladies in the Dumb Shows, Women attending on the Queen, Scribes, Officers, Guards, Attendants, and Six Spirits appearing to Queen Katharine*

CHAPTER NINE

VOCABULARY – PREFIXES, SUFFIXES AND ROOTS

The use and manipulation of vocabulary is the one mental skill which, above all others, can be most closely correlated with general personal success. It is therefore essential, throughout your life, to develop this enticing and personally releasing ability.

This may initially seem a daunting task, but happily there is an easy way to spend a little time in order to gain maximum rewards. In the same way that Meccano and Lego sets use a few basic pieces in order to create an infinity of shapes and structures, so vocabulary is based upon a relatively few prefixes, suffixes and roots.

On the following pages you will find, in order, the major prefixes, suffixes and roots that are liberally sprinkled through *every* conversation you have, or article and book that you read.

By using SEM^3 to remember these key units of vocabulary, you will enhance your memory and your ability to increase your vocabulary and therefore your 'success quotient'. You will have also increased your intelligence, because memory and vocabulary skills are the two main ingredients of standard intelligence (IQ) Tests.

Prefixes

(L = Latin; G = Greek; F = French; E = English)

Prefix	*Meaning*	*Example*
a-, an- (G)	without, not	anaerobic
ab-, abs- (L)	away, from, apart	absent
ad-, ac-, af- (L)	to, towards	advent, advance
aero-	air	aeroplane, aeronaut
amb-, ambi- (G)	both, around	ambiguous
amphi- (G)	both, around	amphitheatre
ante- (L)	before	antenatal
anti- (G)	against	antidote, antitoxic
apo-	away from	apostasy

Prefix	*Meaning*	*Example*
arch- (G)	chief, most important	archbishop, archcriminal
auto- (G)	self	automatic, autocrat
be-	about, make	belittle, beguile, beset
bene- (L)	well, good	benediction
bi- (G)	two	biennial, bicycle
by-, bye- (G)	added to	by ways, by-laws
cata- (G)	down	catalogue, cataract
centi, cente- (L)	hundred	centigrade, centenary
circum- (L)	around	circumference, circumambient
co-, col-, com-, cor-	together	companion
con- (L)	with	collect, co-operate
contra- (L)	against, counter	contradict, contraceptive
de- (F)	down	denude, decentralise
deca-, deci- (G)	ten	decade, decagon
demi- (L)	half	demigod
dia- (G)	through, between	diameter
dis- (L)	not, opposite to	dislike, disagree
duo- (G)	two	duologue, duplex
dys-	ill, hard	dysentery
e-, ex-	out of	exhale, excavate
ec- (L)	out of	eccentric
en-, in-, em-, im-, (L; G) (F)	into, not	enrage, inability, embolden, emulate, impress
epi- (G)	upon, at, in addition	epidemic, epidermis
equi-	equally	equidistant
extra- (L)	outside, beyond	extra-essential
for-, fore- (E)	before	foresee
hemi- (G)	half	hemisphere
hepta- (G)	seven	heptagon
hexa- (G)	six	hexagon, hexateuch
homo- (L)	same	homonym
hyper- (G)	above, excessive	hypercritical, hypertrophy
il-	not	illegal, illogical
in-, im- (un) (L, G, F)	not	imperfect, inaccessible
inter- (L)	among, between	interrupt, intermarriage
intra-, intro- (L)	inside, within	intramural, introvert
iso- (G)	equal, same	isobaric, isosceles
mal- (L)	bad, wrong	malfunction, malformed
meta- (G)	after, beyond	metabolism, metaphysical
mis-	wrongly	misfit, mislead
mono- (G)	one, single	monotonous, monocular
multi- (L)	many	multipurpose, multimillon
non-	not	nonsense, nonpareil
ob-, oc-, of-, op- (L)	in the way of, resistance	obstruct, obstacle, oppose

Prefix	*Meaning*	*Example*
octa-, octo- (G)	eight	octahedron, octave
off-	away, apart	offset
out-	beyond	outnumber, outstanding
over-	above	overhear, overcharge
para- (G)	aside, beyond	parable, paradox
penta- (G)	five	pentagon, pentateuch
per- (L)	through	perennial, peradventure
peri- (G)	around, about	perimeter, pericardium
poly- (G)	many	polygamy, polytechnic
post- (L)	after	postscript, postnatal
pre- (L)	before	prehistoric, pre-war
prime-, primo- (L)	first, important	primary, Prime Minister
pro- (L)	in front of, favouring	prologue, pro-British
quadri- (L)	four	quadriennial, quadrangle
re- (L)	again, back	reappear, recivilise
retro- (L)	backward	retrograde, retrospect
se-	aside	secede
self-	personalising	selfcontrol, selftaught
semi- (G)	half	semicircle, semidetached
sub- (L)	under	submarine, subterranean
super- (L)	above, over	superfluous, superior
syl-	with, together	syllogism
syn, sym- (G)	together	sympathy, synchronise
tele- (G)	far, at or to a distance	telegram, telepathy
ter- (L)	three times	tercentenary
tetra- (G)	four	tetrahedron, tetralogy
trans- (L)	across, through	transatlantic, translate
tri- (L; G)	three	triangle, tripartite
ultra- (L)	beyond	ultramarine, ultra-violet
un- (im) (L, G, F)	not	unbroken, unbutton, unable
under-	below	underfed, underling
uni- (L)	one	unicellular, uniform
vice- (L)	in place of	viceroy, vice-president
yester- (E)	preceding time	yesterday, yesteryear

Suffixes

Suffix	*Meaning*	*Example*
-able, -ible (L)	capable of, fit for	durable, comprehensible
-acy (L; G)	state or quality of	accuracy
-age (L)	action or state of	breakage
-al, -ial (L)	relating to	abdominal
-an (ane, ian) (L)	the nature of	Grecian, African
-ance, ence	quality or action of	insurance, corpulence

Suffix	*Meaning*	*Example*
-ant (L)	forming adjectives of quality, nouns signifying a personal agent or something producing an effect	defiant, servant
-arium, -orium (L)	place for	aquarium, auditorium
-ary (L)	place for, dealing with	seminary, dictionary
-atable (L)	See -able, -ible	
ate (L)	cause to be, office of	animate, magistrate
-ation, -ition (L)	action or state of	condition, dilapidation
-cle, -icle (L)	diminutive	icicle
-dom (E)	condition or control	kingdom
-en (E)	small	mitten
-en (E)	quality	golden, broken
-er (E)	belonging to	farmer, New Yorker
-ess (E)	feminine suffix	hostess, waitress
-et, ette (L)	small	puppet, marionette
-ferous (L)	producing	coniferous
-ful (E)	full of	colourful, beautiful
-fy, ify (L)	make	satisfy, fortify
-hood (E)	state or condition of	boyhood, childhood
-ia (L)	names of classes, names of places	bacteria, America
-ian (L)	practioners or inhabitants	musician, Parisian
-ion (L)	condition or action of	persuasion
-ic (G)	relating to	historic
-id(e) (L)	a quality	acid
-ine (G; L)	a compound	chlorine
-ish (E)	a similarity or relationship	childish, greenish
-ism (G)	quality or doctrine of	realism, socialism
-ist (G)	one who practices	chemist, pessimist
-itis (L)	inflammation of (medical)	bronchitis
-ity, -ety, ty (L)	state or quality of	loyalty
-ive (L)	nature of	creative, receptive
-ize, ise (G)	make, practise, act like	modernize, advertise
-lent (L)	fulness	violent
-less (E)	lacking	fearless, faceless
-logy (G)	indicating a branch of knowledge	biology, psychology
-ly (E)	having the quality of	softly, quickly
-ment (L)	act or condition of	resentment
-metry, -meter (G)	measurement	gasometer, geometry
-mony	resulting condition	testimony

Suffix	*Meaning*	*Example*
-oid (G)	resembling	ovoid
-or (L)	a state or action, a person who, or thing which	error, governor, victor, generator
-osis	process or condition of	metamorphosis
-ous, -ose (L)	full of	murderous, anxious, officious, morose
-some	like	gladsome
-tude (L)	quality or degree of	attitude, gratitude
-ward (E)	direction	backward, outward
-y (E)	condition	difficulty

Roots

Root	*Meaning*	*Example*
aer	air	aerate, aeroplane
am (fr. amare)	love	amorous, amateur, amiable
ann (fr. annus)	year	annual, anniversary
aud, (fr. audire)	hear	auditorium, audit
bio	life	biography
cap (fr. capire)	take	captive
cap (fr. caput)	head	capital, per capita, decapitate
chron	time	chronology, chronic
cor	heart	cordial
corp	body	corporation
de	god	deify, deity
dic, dict	say, speak	dictate
duc, (fr. ducere)	lead	aqueduct, duke, ductile
ego	I	egotism
equi	equal	equidistant
fac, fic, (fr. facere)	make, do	manufacture, efficient
frat	brother	fraternity
geo	earth	geology
graph	write	calligraphy, graphology, telegraph
loc (fr. locus)	place	location, local
loqu, loc (fr. loqui)	speak	eloquence, circumlocution
luc, (fr. lux)	light	elucidate
man (fr. manus)	hand	manuscript, manipulate
mit, miss (fr. mittere)	send	admit, permission
mort, (fr. mors)	death	immortal
omni	all	omnipotent, omnibus
pat (fr. pater)	father	paternal
path	suffering, feeling	sympathy, pathology

Root	*Meaning*	*Example*
ped, (fr. pes)	foot	impede, millepede, pedal
phobia, phobe	fear	hydrophobe, xenophobia
photo	light	photography
pneum	air, breath, spirit	pneumonia
pos, posit	place	deposit, position
pot, poss, poten,		
(fr. ponerte)	be able	potential, possible
quaerere	ask, question, seek	inquiry, query
rog, (fr. rogare)		interrogate
scrib, scrip,	ask	
(fr. scribere)	write	scribble, script, inscribe
sent, sens,		
(fr. sentire)	feel	sensitive, sentiment
sol	alone	soloist, isolate
soph	wise	philosopher
spect, (fr. spicere)	look	introspective, inspect
spir, (fr. spirare)	breathe	inspiration
ten, (fr. tendere)	stretch	extend, tense
ten, (fr. tenere)	hold	tenant
therm, (fr. thermos)	warm	thermometer
utilis	useful	utility
ven, vent (fr. venire)	come, arrive	advent, convenient
vert, vers,		
(fr. vertere)	turn	revert, adverse
vid, vis (fr. videre)	see	supervisor, vision, provident

CHAPTER TEN

LANGUAGES

Fifty percent of all spoken language is composed of one hundred basic key words. For this reason *Master Your Memory* has included the hundred basic words from ten of the world's most common languages.

Applying SEM^3 to languages, you simply mark off one of the thousand cross matrixes, say 5,000 to 5,999, and apply the Memory Principles as before.

For example, if you were going to visit Italy, and wished to learn the first one hundred words of the Italian vocabulary, and were using the Sensation 5,000 Memory Matrix, and were wanting to remember the third word in the list 'tutto', which means 'all', you would take the Key Memory Image 5,003 your mother swimming in an Italian sea or lake. You would *feel* the sensations that your mother feels as she swims and looks around, taking in *ALL* that is moving and going on around her, as you envisage her particularly feeling her *TWO TOES* at the same time!

Memorising vocabulary in this way not only helps you memorise the vocabulary, but helps you also use imagery and sensation, which recent research has discovered are major elements in any successful language learning.

	English	***Italian***	***Italian Pronunciation***
1	After	Dietro	Dee-ay'troh
2	Again	Di nuovo	Dee-noo-oh'voh
3	All	Tutto	Toot'toh
4	Almost	Quasi	Kwah'zee
5	Also	Anche	Ahng'kay
6	Always	Sempre	Sem'pray
7	And	E	Ay
8	A, an	Un, Una	Oon, oona

	English	Italian	Italian Pronunciation
9	Because	Perche	Pehr'kay
10	Before	Davanti	Dah-vahn'tee
11	Big	Grande	Grahn'day
12	But	Ma	Mah
13	Can (I can)	Io posso	Ee'oh poss-oh
14	Come (I Come)	Io vengo	Ee'oh ven'go
15	Either/or	O/o	Oh/oh
16	Find (I find)	Io trovo	Ee'oh troh-voh
17	First	Primo	Pree-moh
18	For	Per	Pehr
19	Friend	Amico	Am-ee'coh
20	From	Da	Dah
21	Go (I go)	Io vado	Ee'oh vah'doh
22	Good	Buono	Boo-oh'noh
23	Goodbye	Arrivederci	Ahr-ree 'veh-dehr' chee
24	Happy	Felice	Fe'lee'cheh
25	Have (I have)	Io ho	Ee'oh ho
26	He	Lui	Loo'ee
27	Hello	Ciao	Chah-oo
28	Here	Qui	Kwee
29	How	Come	Koh'may
30	I	Io	Ee'oh
31	I am	Sono	Soh'noh
32	If	Se	Say
33	In	In	Een
34	Know (I know)	Io conosco	Ee'oh koh-noh-sho
35	Last	Scorso	Skorr'soh
36	Like (I like)	Mi piace	Mee pee-ah' chay
37	Little	Poco	Poh'koh
38	Love (I love)	Io amo	Eeh'oh am'oh
39	Make (I make)	Io faccio	Ee'oh fas'chee-oh
40	Many	Molti	Moll-tee
41	Me	Mi	May
42	More	Piu	Pee'oo
43	Most	Il piu	Eel pee'oo
44	Much	Molto	Moll'toh
45	My	Mio	Mee'oh
46	New	Nuovo	Noo-oh'voh
47	No	No	Noh
48	Not	Non	Nonn
49	Now	Ora	Oh'rah

	English	Italian	Italian Pronunciation
50	Of	Di	Dee
51	Often	Spesso	Spess'soh
52	On	Su	Soo
53	One	Uno	Oon'oh
54	Only	Solo	Soh'loh
55	Or	O	Oh
56	Other	Altro	Ahl'troh
57	Our	Il nostro	Eel noss'troh
58	Out	Fuori	Foo-oh'ree
59	Over	Attraverso	Aht'trah-vehr'soh
60	People	Gente	Jen'tay
61	Place	Luogo	Loo-oh'goh
62	Please	Per favore	Pehr fah-voh'ray
63	Same	Medesimo	May-day'zeemoh
64	See (I see)	Io vedo	Eeh'oh vay-doh
65	She	Lei	Lay'ee
66	So	Cosi	Koh'see
67	Some	Qualche	Kwahl'kay
68	Sometimes	Talvolta	Tahl-voll'tah
69	Still	Ancora	Ahng'koh-rah
70	Such	Tale	Tah'lay
71	Tell (I tell)	Io racconto	Ee'oh rak-kohn'toh
72	Thank you	Grazie	Grah'tsee
73	That	Quello	Kwell'loh
74	The	Il, la	Eel, lah
75	Their	Il loro, la loro	Eel loh'roh, lah loh'roh
76	Them	Li, le, loro	Lee, lay, loh'roh
77	Then	Allora	Ahl-loh'rah
78	There is, There are	C'e, ci sono	Chay, chee soh-noh
79	They	Loro	Loh'roh
80	Thing	Cosa	Koh'sah
81	Think (I think)	Io penso	Eeh'oh pen-soh
82	This	Questo	Kwess'toh
83	Time	Ora	Oh'rah
84	To	Per	Pehr
85	Under	Piu basso	Pee-oo bahs'soh
86	Up	Su per	Soo pehr
87	Us	Noi	Noh'ee
88	Use (I use)	Io uso	Eeh'oh oo-zoh
89	Very	Molto	Moll'toh
90	We	Noi	Noh'ee
91	What	Come	Koh'may

	English	Italian	Italian Pronunciation
92	When	Quando	Kwahn'doh
93	Where	Dove	Doh'vay
94	Which	Quale	Kwah'lay
95	Who	Chi	Kee
96	Why	Perche	Pehr-kay
97	With	Con	Kon
98	Yes	Si	See
99	You	Tu	Too
100	Your	Il suo, la sua	Eel soo'oh, lah soo'ah

	English	French	French Pronunciation
1	After	Apres	A'pray
2	Again	Encore	O(n)'kor
3	All	Tout, toute	Too, toot
4	Almost	Presque	Press'ke
5	Also	Aussi	Oh'see
6	Always	Toujours	Too'shure
7	And	Et	Ay
8	A, an	Un, une	Er(n), oon
9	Because	Parce que	Pah'ske
10	Before	Avant	A'vo(n)
11	Big	Grand	Gro(n)
12	But	Mais	May
13	Can (I can)	Je peux	*Je pe
14	Come (I Come)	Je viens	*Je vee'a(n)
15	Either/or	Ou/ou	Ooh/ooh
16	Find (I find)	Je trouve	*Je troov
17	First	Premier	Preh'mee'ay
18	For	Pour	Poor
19	Friend	Ami	Am'ee
20	From	De	De
21	Go (I go)	Je vais	*Je vay
22	Good	Bien	Bee'a(n)
23	Goodbye	Au revoir	O-re'vwa
24	Happy	Content	Ko(n)'to(n)
25	Have (I have)	J'ai	*Jay
26	He	Il	Eel
27	Hello	Bonjour	Bo(n)'shure
28	Here	Ici	Ee'see
29	How	Comment	Kom'o(n)

	English	French	French Pronunciation
30	I	Je	*Je
31	I am	Je suis	*Je swee
32	If	Si	See
33	In	Dans	Do(n)
34	Know (I know)	Je sais	*Je say
35	Last	Dernier	Dair'nee'ay
36	Like (I like)	J'aime	*Jem
37	Little	Petit	Pe'tee
38	Love (I love)	J'aime	*Jem
39	Make (I make)	Je fais	*Je fay
40	Many	Beaucoup	Bo' ku
41	Me	Moi	Mwa
42	More	Plus	Ploo
43	Most	La plupart	La ploo'par
44	Much	Beaucoup	Bo'ku
45	My	Mon	Mo(n)
46	New	Nouveau, nouvelle	Nu'vo, nu'vel
47	No	Non	No(n)
48	Not	Ne pas	Ne pah
49	Now	Maintenant	Ma(n)'te'no(n)
50	Of	De	De
51	Often	Souvent	Soo'von(n)
52	On	Sur	S'ure
53	One	Un	Er(n)
54	Only	Seulement	Serl'e'mo(n)
55	Or	Ou	Ooh
56	Other	Autre	Oh'tr
57	Our	Notre	No'tr
58	Out	Dehors	De'or
59	Over	Pardessus	Par'de'soo
60	People	Les gens	Lay *jo(n)
61	Place	Place	Plas
62	Please	S'il vous plait	See voo play
63	Same	Meme	Memm
64	See (I see)	Je vois	*Je vwa
65	She	Elle	El
66	So	Donc	Do(n)k
67	Some	Quelque	Kel'ke
68	Sometimes	Quelquefois	Kel'ke fwa
69	Still	Encore	O(n)'kor
70	Such	Tel	Tell
71	Tell (I tell)	Je dis	*Je dee
72	Thank you	Merci	Mair'see

	English	French	French Pronunciation
73	That	Que	Ke
74	The	Le, la	Le, lah
75	Their	Leur	Ler
76	Them	Les	Lay
77	Then	Alors	Ahl-loh're
78	There is, There are	Il y a	Eel ee ar
79	They	Ils, elles	Eel, ell
80	Thing	Chose	Sh'ohs
81	Think (I think)	Je pense	*Je po(n)se
82	This	Ce, cette	Se, set
83	Time	Temps	To(n)
84	To	A	Ah
85	Under	Sous	Soo
86	Up	En haut	On'oh
87	Us	Nous	Noo
88	Use (I use)	J'utilise	*Joo'tee'lees
89	Very	Tres	Tray
90	We	Nous	Noo
91	What	Que	Ke
92	When	Quand	Ko(n)
93	Where	Ou	Ooh
94	Which	Qui	Kee
95	Who	Qui	Kee
96	Why	Pourquoi	Poor kwah
97	With	Avec	A'vek
98	Yes	Oui	Wee
99	You	Tu, vous	Too, voo
100	Your	Ton, tes, votre, vos	To(n), tay, vot're, voh

NOTES:
French pronunciation: *Je is pronounced like (plea)sure or (bei)ge; where n is in brackets (n) pronounced nasally.

	English	German	German Pronunciation
1	After	Nach	Nahk
2	Again	Wieder	Vee-dair
3	All	Alle	Ul-le
4	Almost	Beinahe	By-nah
5	Also	Auch	Owk
6	Always	Immer	Im'me
7	And	Und	Oont

	English	*German*	*German Pronunciation*
8	A, an	Ein, eine	Ine, i-ne
9	Because	Weil	Vile
10	Before	Vorn	Fawn
11	Big	Gross	Grohs
12	But	Aber	Arb'e
13	Can (I can)	Ich kann	Ik kan
14	Come (I Come)	Ich komme	Ik komm'e
15	Either/or	Entweder/oder	Ent'vay'de/oh'de
16	Find (I find)	Ich finde	Ik fin'de
17	First	Erst	Air'st
18	For	Fur	Fewr
19	Friend	Freund	Froynt
20	From	Von	Fon
21	Go (I go)	Ich gehe	Ik gay'e
22	Good	Gut	Goot
23	Goodbye	Auf wiedersehen	Owf'vee'dair-zay-en
24	Happy	Froh	Fro
25	Have (I have)	Ich habe	Ik hah'be
26	He	Er	Air
27	Hello	Guten tag	Goot'en tahg
28	Here	Hier	Heer
29	How	Wie	Vee
30	I	Ich	Ik
31	I am	Ich bin	Ik bin
32	If	Wenn	Ven
33	In	In	In
34	Know (I know)	Ich weiss	Ik vice
35	Last	Letzt	Let's't
36	Like (I like)	Ich liebe	Ik lee'be
37	Little	Klein	Kline
38	Love (I love)	Ich liebe	Ik lee'be
39	Make (I make)	Ich Mache	Ik mu'ke
40	Many	Viel	Feel
41	Me	Mich	Mik
42	More	Mehr	M'air
43	Most	Die meisten	Dee my'sten
44	Much	Viel	Feel
45	My	Mein	Mine
46	New	Neu	Noy
47	No	Nein	Nine
48	Not	Nicht	Nikt
49	Now	Jetzt	Yet's't
50	Of	Von	Fon

	English	German	German Pronunciation
51	Often	Oft	Off't
52	On	Auf	Owf
53	One	Ein	Ine
54	Only	Nur	Newr
55	Or	Oder	O'de
56	Other	Andere	Un'de're
57	Our	Unser	Oon'sair
58	Out	Aus	Ows
59	Over	Uber	Oo'bair
60	People	Leute	Loy'te
61	Place	Platz	Plahts
62	Please	Bitte	Bitter
63	Same	Derselbe, dieselbe, dasselbe	Dair'sel'be, dee'sel'be, duss'sel'be
64	See (I see)	Ich sehe	Ik say'e
65	She	Sie	Zee
66	So	So	Zoh
67	Some	Etwas	Et'vahss
68	Sometimes	Manchmal	Monk'mahl
69	Still	Noch	Nok
70	Such	Solch	Solk
71	Tell (I tell)	Ich erzahle	Ik air'zay'le
72	Thank you	Danke	Dahnn'ke
73	That	Das	Duss
74	The	Der, die, das	Dair, dee, duss
75	Their	Ihr	Eer
76	Them	Sie	Zee
77	Then	Dann	Dahnn
78	There is, There are	Es gibt	Ess gib't
79	They	Sie	Zee
80	Thing	Die sache	Dee sah'ke
81	Think (I think)	Ich denke	Ik den'ke
82	This	Diese	Dee'ze
83	Time	Zeit	Tsite
84	To	Nach	Nahk
85	Under	Unter	Oon'te
86	Up	Auf	Ow'f
87	Us	Uns	Oon's
88	Use (I use)	Ich gebrauche	Ik gay'brow'ke
89	Very	Sehr	Zare
90	We	Wir	Veer
91	What	Wass	Vahss

	English	German	German Pronunciation
92	When	Wann	Vun
93	Where	Wo	Voh
94	Which	Welche	Vel'ke
95	Who	Wer	Vair
96	Why	Warum	Var'oom
97	With	Mit	Mitt
98	Yes	Ja	Yah
99	You	Du, sie	Doo, zee
100	Your	Ihr, Euer	Eer, oy'e

NOTES:
German pronunciation: OW as in COW; G as in Goat; K as in loCH; U as in Up.

	English	Portuguese	Portuguese Pronunciation
1	After	Depois	De-poh'eesh
2	Again	De novo	De-no'voo
3	All	Todo	Toh'doo
4	Almost	Quase	Kwah'ze
5	Also	Tambem	Tan-ben
6	Always	Sempre	Sen'pre
7	And	E	Ee
8	A, an	Um, uma	Oon, oona
9	Because	Porque	Poor'ke
10	Before	Antes	Antsh
11	Big	Grande	Grand
12	But	Mas	Mash
13	Can (I can)	Posso	Possoh
14	Come (I Come)	Venho	Vain'yoh
15	Either/or	Um ou outro	Oon oh oh'troo
16	Find (I find)	Acho	Ash'oh
17	First	Primeiro	Pri-may'ee-roo
18	For	Para	Pa'ra
19	Friend		
20	From	De	Deh
21	Go (I go)	Vou	Vor
22	Good	Bom	Bon
23	Goodbye	Adeus	A-day'oosh
24	Happy		
25	Have (I have)	Tenho	Tain'yoh
26	He	Ele	El'ay

	English	Portuguese	Portuguese Pronunciation
27	Hello	Ola	O-lah
28	Here	Aqui	A-kee
29	How	Como	Coh'moh
30	I	Eu	Eh'oh
31	I am	Sou	Sue
32	If	Se	Seh
33	In	Em	En
34	Know (I know)	Conheco	Con'ye'soh
35	Last	Ultimo	Ool'tee-moo
36	Like (I like)	Gosto	Gos'toh
37	Little	Pequeno	Pe-kay'noo
38	Love (I love)		
39	Make (I make)	Faco	Fuss'oo
40	Many	Muitos	Mween'toos
41	Me	Me	Meh
42	More	Mais	My'sh
43	Most	O mais	Ooh my'sh
44	Much	Muito	Mween'too
45	My	Meu	May'oo
46	New	Novo	Noh'voo
47	No	Nao	Nown
48	Not	Nao	Nown
49	Now	Agora	A-go'ra
50	Of	De	Deh
51	Often	Muitas vezes	Mwee'tas vay'ze
52	On	Sobre	Soh'breh
53	One	Um, uma	Oon, oona
54	Only	Unico	Oo'nee-koo
55	Or	Ou	Oh
56	Other	Outro	Oh-troo
57	Our	Nosso	Nos'soh
58	Out	Fora	Fo'ra
59	Over	Sobre	Soh'breh
60	People	Gente	Zhent
61	Place	Lugar	Loo-gar
62	Please	Faca favor	Fassa fa-vohr
63	Same	Mesmo	Mayzh'moo
64	See (I see)	Vejo	Vay'yoh
65	She	Ela	Ella
66	So	Tao	Town
67	Some	Algum	Al-goon
68	Sometimes	Algumas vezes	Al'goo'mas vay'ze
69	Still	Mas	Mash

	English	Portuguese	Portuguese Pronunciation
70	Such	Tal	Tal
71	Tell (I tell)	Digo	Dee'goo
72	Thank you	Obrigado	Oh-bree-gah'doo
73	That	Aquele	A'kay'le
74	The	O' a	Oh, ah
75	Their	Deles, delas, seu	Del'lays, del'lass, say'oo
76	Them	Os, as	Ohs, ass
77	Then	Depois	De-poh'eesh
78	There is, There are	Ha	Ha
79	They	Eles, elas	El'ays, el'ass
80	Thing	Coisa	Koh'ee-za
81	Think (I think)	Julgo	Yulgo
82	This	Este, esta	Aysht, esh'ta
83	Time	Tempo	Ten'poo
84	To	Para	Pa'ra
85	Under	Sob	Sohb
86	Up	Acima	A-see'ma
87	Us	Nos	Noh's
88	Use (I use)	Uso	Yoo'soh
89	Very	Muito	Mween'too
90	We	Nos	Noss
91	What	O que	Oh ke
92	When	Quando	Kwan'doo
93	Where	Onde	Ond
94	Which	Que	Ke
95	Who	Quem	Kayn
96	Why	Porque	Poor'ke
97	With	Com	Kon
98	Yes	Sim	Seen
99	You	Voce	Vo-say
100	Your	O seu	Oh say'oo

	English	Spanish	Spanish Pronunciation
1	After	Despues	Days-pues
2	Again	De nuevo	Day nway'vo
3	All	Todo	To'do
4	Almost	Casi	Ka'see
5	Also	Tambien	Tam-byayn
6	Always	Siempre	Syem'pray

	English	Spanish	Spanish Pronunciation
7	And	Y	Ee
8	A, an	Un, uno, una	Oon, oo'no, oo'na
9	Because	Porque	Por'kay
10	Before	Ante	An'tay
11	Big	Grande	Gran'day
12	But	Pero	Pay'ro
13	Can (I can)	Puedo	Pway'do
14	Come (I Come)	Vengo	Ven'go
15	Either/or	O/o	Oh/oh
16	Find (I find)	Encuentro	En-kwen'tro
17	First	Primero	Pree-may'ro
18	For	Por	Por
19	Friend	Amigo	Ah'mee-goa
20	From	De	Day
21	Go (I go)	Voy	Voy
22	Good	Bueno	Bway'no
23	Goodbye	Adios	Ah'dyos
24	Happy	Contento	Cont'ten'to
25	Have (I have)	Tengo	Tayn-go
26	He	El	Ell
27	Hello	Buenas dias	Bway'nas dee'as
28	Here	Aqui	Ah-kee
29	How	Como	Ko'mo
30	I	Yo	Yo
31	I am	Soy	Soy
32	If	Si	See
33	In	En	En
34	Know (I know)	Sabo	Sa-bo
35	Last	Ultimo	Ool'tee-mo
36	Like (I like)	Gusto	Goos-to
37	Little	Poco	Po'ko
38	Love (I love)	Amo	Ah'mo
39	Make (I make)	Hago	Ar'go
40	Many	Muchos	Moo'chos
41	Me	Me	May
42	More	Mas	Mas
43	Most	Lo mas	Lo mas
44	Much	Mucho	Moo'cho
45	My	Mi	Mee
46	New	Nuevo	Nway'vo
47	No	No	No
48	Not	No	No
49	Now	Ahora	Ah-o'ra

	English	*Spanish*	*Spanish Pronunciation*
50	Of	De	Day
51	Often	Frecuentemente	Fray-kwen'tay' men'tay
52	On	Sobre	So'bray
53	One	Uno	Oo'no
54	Only	Solo	So'lo
55	Or	O	O
56	Other	Otro	O'tro
57	Our	Nuestro	Nway'stro
58	Out	Fuera	Fway'ra
59	Over	Sobre	So'bray
60	People	Gente	Hen'tay
61	Place	Lugar	Loo-gar
62	Please	Por favor	Por fa'vor
63	Same	Mismo	Mees'mo
64	See (I see)	Veo	Vay'o
65	She	Ella	El'lya
66	So	Asi	Ah-see
67	Some	Algun	Al-goon
68	Sometimes	Alguna vez	Al-goo'na vayth
69	Still	Siempre	Syem'pray
70	Such	Tal	Tal
71	Tell (I tell)	Digo	Dee'go
72	Thank you	Gracias	Gra'thyas
73	That	Ese	Ay'say
74	The	El, la, lo	Ayl, lah, loh
75	Their	Su, sus	Soo, soos
76	Them	Los, las, les	Los, lahss, lays
77	Then	Luego	Lway'go
78	There is, There are	Hay	Ahy
79	They	Ellos, ellas	Ay'lyos, Ay,lyahss
80	Thing	Cosa	Ko'sa
81	Think (I think)	Pienso	Pyayn-so
82	This	Este, esta	Ays'tay, ays'tah
83	Time	Tiempo	Tyem'po
84	To	A	Ah
85	Under	Debajo	Day-ba'ho
86	Up	Arriba	Ah-ree'ba
87	Us	Nos	Nohs
88	Use (I use)	Uso	Oo'so
89	Very	Mismo	Mees'mo
90	We	Nosotros	Nohs'ot'rohs
91	What	Lo que	Lo kay

	English	Spanish	Spanish Pronunciation
92	When	Cuando	Kwan'do
93	Where	Donde	Don'day
94	Which	Que	Kay
95	Who	Quien	Kee'en
96	Why	Porque	Por'kay
97	With	Con	Kon
98	Yes	Si	See
99	You	Tu	Too
100	Your	Suyo	Soo'yo

	English	Russian	Russian Pronunciation
1	After	Posle	Poh'slye
2	Again	Eshche	Yesh-cho'
3	All	Vse	Fsye
4	Almost	Pochti	Puhch-tee
5	Also	Tozhe	Toh'zhe
6	Always	Vsegda	Fsyeg-da'
7	And	I	Ee
8	A, an	–	–
9	Because	Potomu Chto	Puh-tuh-moo' shto
10	Before	Do	Doh
11	Big	Bolshoi	Buhl-shoi
12	But	No	No
13	Can (I can)	Ya mogu	Ya muh-goo
14	Come (I Come)	Ya pridu	Yah pree-doo
15	Either/or	Ili/ili	Ee'li/ee'li
16	Find (I find)	Ya naidu	Ya nuhee-doo
17	First	Pervyi	Pyehr'vooi
18	For	Dlya	Dlyah
19	Friend	Dryg	Droog
20	From	Ot	Ot
21	Go (I go)	Ya idu	Ya ee-doo'
22	Good	Khorosho	Khu-ruh-shoh'
23	Goodbye	Do svidaniya	Duh-svi-dan'yuh
24	Happy	Schastlivyi	Schuhst-lee'-vooi
25	Have (I have)	Ya imeyu	Ya eem-yay'yoo
26	He	On	Ohn
27	Hello	Sdravstvuite	Zdrafst'vooi-tye
28	Here	Zdes	Zdyays
29	How	Kak	Kak

	English	Russian	Russian Pronunciation
30	I	Ya	Yah
31	I am	Ya	Yah
32	If	Esli	Yasy'lee
33	In	V	V
34	Know (I know)	Ya znayu	Yah Znaee'yoo
35	Last	Poslednii	Puh'slyay'dnee
36	Like (I like)	Mne Nravitsya	Mnye nra'vi-tsyuh
37	Little	Malenkii	Ma'lyen-kee
38	Love (I love)	Ya lyublyu	Ya lyoob-lyoo'
39	Make (I make)	Ya delayu	Ya dyehl'-yoo
40	Many	Mnogo	Mnoh'gol
41	Me	Menya	Men-yah
42	More	Bolshe	Bol'she
43	Most	Nai-bolshii	Nai-bol'shee
44	Much	Mnogo	Mnoh'goh
45	My	Moi	Mo'ee
46	New	Novyi	Noh'vooee
47	No	Net	Nyet
48	Not	Ne	Nye
49	Now	Teper	Tye-pyehr'
50	Of	Iz	Is
51	Often	Chasto	Chuh'stoh
52	On	Na	Nah
53	One	Odin	Uh-deen
54	Only	Tolko	Tohl'koh
55	Or	Ili	Ee'li
56	Other	Drugoi	Droo-goy
57	Our	Nash	Nahsh
58	Out	Iz	Is
59	Over	Nad	Nahd
60	People	Lyudi	Lyoo'dee
61	Place	Mesto	Myes'tuh
62	Please	Pozhaluista	Puh-zhahl'stah
63	Same	Samyi	Sahm'ooee
64	See (I see)	Ya Vizhu	Yah vee'zhoo
65	She	Ona	Uh-nah
66	So	Tak	Tuhk
67	Some	Nekotoryi	Nye'kuh-to-rooi
68	Sometimes	Inogda	Ee-nuhg-dah
69	Still	Eschcho	Yesh-choh'
70	Such	Takoi	Tuh-koy
71	Tell (I tell)	Ya skazhu	Yaskuh-zhoo'
72	Thank you	Spasibo	Spuh-see'buh

	English	Russian	Russian Pronunciation
73	That	Etot	Eh'tuht
74	The	–	–
75	Their	Ikh	Eekh
76	Them	Ikh	Eekh
77	Then	Togda	Tuhg-dah
78	There is, There are	Est	Yest
79	They	Oni	Uh-nee
80	Thing	Predmet	Pryed-myet'
81	Think (I think)	Ya dumayu	Yah doo'mah-yoo
82	This	Etot	Eh'tuht
83	Time	Vremya	Vry-ay'myuh
84	To	Na	Nah
85	Under	Pod	Pod
86	Up	Naverkh	Nah-vehrkh
87	Us	Nas	Nahs
88	Use (I use)	Ya ispolzuyu	Ya is-pol'zoo-yoo
89	Very	Ochen	Oh'chen
90	We	Myi	Mooee
91	What	Chto	Shtoh
92	When	Kogda	Kuhg-dah
93	Where	Gde	Gdye
94	Which	Kakoi	Kuh-koi'
95	Who	Kto	Ktoh
96	Why	Pochemu	Puh-che-moo'
97	With	S	S
98	Yes	Da	Dah
99	You	Vyi	Vooee
100	Your	Vash	Vahsh

NOTES:
Russian pronunciation: ' at the end of the stressed syllable

KH	as in Scottish loCH	EH	as in hAIr
ZH	as in pleasSure	O	as in dOck
A	as in cAr	OH	as in ORder
E	as in bEt	UH	a in dUck

OOI a single sound with the emphasis on the 'i'

	English	Swedish	Swedish Pronunciation
1	After	Efter	Ef'ter
2	Again	Igen	Ee-yan
3	All	All	Al
4	Almost	Naestan	Nast-an

	English	*Swedish*	*Swedish Pronunciation*
5	Also	Ocksaa	Oxo
6	Always	Alltid	Ull-tid
7	And	Och	Ok
8	A, an	En, ett	En, et
9	Because	Daerfoer att	Dair-fuhr art
10	Before	Innan	In-nan
11	Big	Stor	Storr
12	But	Men	Men
13	Can (I can)	Jag kan	Jarg kan
14	Come (I Come)	Jag kommer	Jarg kom-merr
15	Either/or	Antingen/eller	An-ting-en/ell-err
16	Find (I find)	Jag finner	Jarg fin-nerr
17	First	Foerst	Firsht
18	For	Foer	Furr
19	Friend	Vaen	Ven
20	From	Fraan	Frorn
21	Go (I go)	Jag ga	Jarg gor
22	Good	Bra	Bra
23	Goodbye	Adjoe	Ad-jo
24	Happy	Glad	Glard
25	Have (I have)	Jag har	Jarg harr
26	He	Han	Hun
27	Hello	Goddag	Go-darg
28	Here	Haer	Harr
29	How	Hur	Hoorr
30	I	Jag	Jarg
31	I am	Jag aer	Jarg arr
32	If	Om	Om
33	In	I	Ee
34	Know (I know)	Jag kan	Jarg kan
35	Last	Foerra	For-rah
36	Like (I like)	Jag tycker om	Jarg tickerr om
37	Little	Liten, Litet	Litten, littett
38	Love (I love)	Jag Aelskar	Jarg elskarr
39	Make (I make)	Jag gara	Jarg gor'ra
40	Many	Manga	Mong'a
41	Me	Mig	May
42	More	Mera	Meer-ra
43	Most	Mest	Mest
44	Much	Mycket	Micket
45	My	Min, Mitt	Min, mitt
46	New	Ny	Nu
47	No	Nej	Nay

	English	Swedish	Swedish Pronunciation
48	Not	Inte	Inter
49	Now	Nu	Nu
50	Of	Av	Arv
51	Often	Ofta	Ofta
52	On	Paa	Por
53	One	En, ett, man	En, ett, man
54	Only	Bara	Bar'ra
55	Or	Eller	Ellerr
56	Other	Annan, Annat	Annan, annat
57	Our	Vaar, Vaart, Vaara	Vorr, vorrt, vorr'ah
58	Out	Ut	Uut
59	Over	Over	Er-ver
60	People	Folk	Folk
61	Place	Plats	Plats
62	Please	Varsaagod	Vor-so-good
63	Same	Samma	Sam'ma
64	See (I see)	Jag ser	Jarg seer
65	She	Hon	Hon
66	So	Saa	Sor
67	Some	Naagon, Naagot, Naagra	No'gon, No'got, No'grra
68	Sometimes	Ibland	Ee'bland
69	Still	Aendaa	An'dor
70	Such	Saadan	Sor'dan
71	Tell (I tell)	Jag beratta	Jarg be'ra'tar
72	Thank you	Tack	Tack
73	That	Att	At
74	The	–	–
75	Their	Deras	Dair'as
76	Them	Dem	Dem
77	Then	Daa	Dor
78	There is, There are	Det finns, det ar	Det fins, det air
79	They	De	Dear
80	Thing	Sak	Sark
81	Think (I think)	Jag tror	Jarg trorr
82	This	Denna, detta	Denna, detta
83	Time	Tid	Teed
84	To	Till	Till
85	Under	Under	Onderr
86	Up	Upp	Opp
87	Us	Oss	Oss
88	Use (I use)	Jag anvaender	Jarg an'van-derr
89	Very	Mycket	Micket

	English	Swedish	Swedish Pronunciation
90	We	Vi	Vee
91	What	Vad	Vard
92	When	Naer	Nair
93	Where	Var	Varr
94	Which	Vilken	Vil'ken
95	Who	Vem	Vem
96	Why	Varfor	Varr'fuhr
97	With	Med	Maird
98	Yes	Ja	Ja
99	You	Du, ni	Duu, nee
100	Your	Din, ditt	Din, ditt

NOTES ON SWEDISH TRANSLATION
AA=Å
AE=Ä
OE=Ö

	English	Chinese Chinese	Chinese (Pin Yin) Pronunciation
1	A, an	Yi ge	Ee ger
2	After	Guo le	Gwo ler
3	Again	You	Yoh
4	All	Dou	Doh
5	Almost	Cha bu duo	Chah boo dwoh
6	Also	Hai	High
7	Always	Yong yuan	Yung yooen
8	And	He	Her
9	Because	Yin wei	Yin way
10	Before	Yi gian	Ee chyen
11	Big	Da	Dah
12	But	Ke shi	Ker shir
13	Can (I can)	Ke yi	Ke ee
14	Come (I Come)	Wo lai	Woh lih
15	Either/or	Huo zhe	Hwoh je
16	Find (I find)	Wo zhao dao	Woh jow dao
17	First	Di yi	Dee ee
18	For	Wei	Way
19	Friend	Peng you	Pung yo
20	From	Cong	Tsong
21	Go (I go)	Wo qu	Woh chew
22	Good	Hao	How
23	Goodbye	Zai jian	Dzih jyen
24	Happy	Gao xing	Gow sing

	English	Chinese Chinese	Chinese (Pin Yin) Pronunciation
25	Have (I have)	Wo you	Woh yo
26	He	Ta	Tah
27	Hello	Ni hao	Nee ow
28	Here	Zhe li	Jer lee
29	How	Zen me	Dzen mer
30	I	Wo	Woh
31	I am	Wo shi	Woh she
32	If	Ru guo	Rroo gwoh
33	In	Li	Lee
34	Know (I know)	Wo zhi dao	Woh jir dow
35	Last	Zui hou	Dzway hoh
36	Like (I like)	Wo xi huan	Woh see hwan
37	Little	Xiao	Seeow
38	Love (I love)	Wo ai	Woh ih
39	Make (I make)	Wo zhi zao	Wo jir dzow
40	Many	Duo	Dwoh
41	Me	Wo	Woh
42	More	Geng duo de	Geung dwor der
43	Most	Zui duo	Dzway dwoh
44	Much	Duo	Dwoh
45	My	Wo de	Woh de
46	New	Xin	Sin
47	No	Bu	Boo
48	Not	Bu shi	Boo shir
49	Now	Xian zai	See'en tsih
50	Of	De	De
51	Often	Jing chang	Jing chung
52	On	Shang	Shung
53	One	Yi	Ee
54	Only	Zhi	Je
55	Or	Huo zhe	Hwor jer
56	Other	Bie de	Beeye de
57	Our	Wo men de	Woh men de
58	Out	Wai	Wih
59	Over	Shang	Shung
60	People	Ren min	Ren min
61	Place	Di fang	Dee fang
62	Please	Qing	Ching
63	Same	Tong	Tung
64	See (I see)	Wo kan jian	Woh kan jyen
65	She	Ta	Tah
66	So	Suo yi	Soowoh ee

	English	Chinese Chinese	Chinese (Pin Yin) Pronunciation
67	Some	Yi xie	Ee sye
68	Sometimes	You shi huo	Yoh she hwoh
69	Still	Hai	Hih
70	Such	Na me	Nah me
71	Tell (I tell)	Wo gao su	Woh gow soo
72	Thank you	Xie xie	Sye sye
73	That	Na ge	Nah ge
74	The	–	–
75	Their	Ta men de	Tah men de
76	Them	Ta men	Tah men
77	Then	Ran hou	Rran hoh
78	There is, There are	You	Yoh
79	They	Ta men	Tah men
80	Thing	Dong xi	Dung see
81	Think (I think)	Xiang	Seeyang
82	This	Zhei ge	Jay ge
83	Time	Shi jian	She jen
84	To	Dao	Dow
85	Under	Xia	Seeah
86	Up	Shang	Shung
87	Us	Wo men	Woh men
88	Use (I use)	Wo yong	Woh yoong
89	Very	Hen	Hen
90	We	Wo men	Woh men
91	What	Shen me	Shen mer
92	When	Shen me shi hou	Shen mer shir ho
93	Where	Zai nar	Tsih nar
94	Which	Nei ge	Nay ger
95	Who	Shei	Shay
96	Why	Wei shi me	Way shir mer
97	With	Tong	Tung
98	Yes	Shi	She
99	You	Ni	Nee
100	Your	Ni de	Nee de

NOTES:

Chinese pronunciation:

OW as in cOW
IH as in hIGH
ER as in hER
IR as in sIR
G as an initial is hard

	English	Japanese	Japanese Pronunciation
1	A, an	Hitotsu no	Hee-toh-tsoo noh
2	After	Atode	Ah-toh-deh
3	Again	Mata	Mah-tah
4	All	Minna	Meen-nah
5	Almost	Hotondo	Hoh-tohn-doh
6	Also	Mata	Mah-tah
7	Always	Itsumo	Ee-tsoo-moh
8	And	Soshite	Soh-shee-teh
9	Because	Node	Noh-deh
10	Before	Mae ni	Mah-eh nee
11	Big	Okii	Oh-kee
12	But	Keredomo	Keh-reh-doh-moh
13	Can (I can)	Dekiru	Deh-kee-doo
14	Come (I Come)	Kuru	Koo-doo
15	Either/or	Ka	Kah
16	Find (I find)	Mitsukeru	Mee-tsoo-keh-doo
17	First	Hajime	Hah-jee-meh
18	For	Tamini	Tah-mee-nee
19	Friend	Tomodachi	Tomo-dar'chee
20	From	Kara	Kah-dah
21	Go (I go)	Ikimasu	Ikki'muss
22	Good	Ii	Ee
23	Goodbye	Sayonara	Sah-yoh-nah-dah
24	Happy	Shiawase	Shee'a-wah'say
25	Have (I have)	Motte imasu	Moht-teh ee-mahss
26	He	Kare	Kah-deh
27	Hello	Konnichi wa	Kohn-nee-chee wah
28	Here	Koko	Koh-koh
29	How	Doshite	Doh'shtey
30	I	Watashi	Wah-tah-shee
31	I am	Watashi wa	Wah-tah-shee wah
32	If	Moshi	Moh-shee
33	In	Ni	Nee
34	Know (I know)	Shitte imasu	Sheet-teh ee-mahss
35	Last	Owari	Oh-wah-dee
36	Like (I like)	Suki	Soo-kee
37	Little	Chiisai	Chee-sah-ee
38	Love (I love)	Sukidesu	Soo'kee-dess'oo
39	Make (I make)	Shitemasu	Shih'ti-muss
40	Many	Takusan	Tah-koo-sahn
41	Me	Watashi ni	Wah-tah-shee nee
42	More	Motto	Moht-toh
43	Most	Ichidan	Ee-chee-dahn

	English	Japanese	Japanese Pronunciation
44	Much	Takusan	Tah-koo-sahn
45	My	Watashi no	Wah-tah-she noh
46	New	Atarashii	Ah-tah-dah-shee
47	No	Iie	Ee-eh
48	Not	Shinai	Shee-nah-ee
49	Now	Ima	Ee-mah
50	Of	No	Noh
51	Often	Tabitabi	Tah-bee-tah-bee
52	On	Ue	Oo-eh
53	One	Ichi	Ee-chee
54	Only	Tatta	Taht-tah
55	Or	Ka	Kah
56	Other	Hoka	Hoh-kah
57	Our	Watatshitachi no	Wah-tah-shee-tah-chee noh
58	Out	Soto	Soh-toh
59	Over	Ue	Oo-eh
60	People	Hitobito	Hee-toh-bee-toh
61	Place	Tokoro	Toh-koh-doh
62	Please	Kudasai	Koo-dah-sich
63	Same	Onaji	Oh-noh-jee
64	See (I see)	Mimasu	Mee-mahss
65	She	Kanojo	Kah-noh-joh
66	So	So	Soh
67	Some	Ikuraka	Ee-koo-dah-kah
68	Sometimes	Tokidoki	Toh-kee-doh-kee
69	Still	Mada	Mah-dah
70	Such	Sonna	Sohn-nah
71	Tell (I tell)	Iiamasu	Ee'muss
72	Thank you	Arigato	Ah-dee-gah-toh
73	That	Sono	Soh-noh
74	The	Sono	Soh-noh
75	Their	Karera no	Kah-deh-dah noh
76	Them	Karera no	Kah-deh-dah noh
77	Then	Dewa	Deh-wah
78	There is, There are	Soko desu	Soh-koh dess
79	They	Karera	Kah-deh-dah
80	Thing	Mono	Moh-noh
81	Think (I think)	Omou	Oh-moh-oo
82	This	Kono	Koh-noh
83	Time	Jikan	Jee-kahn
84	To	Ni	Nee
85	Under	Shita	Shee-tah

	English	Japanese	Japanese Pronunciation
86	Up	Ue	Oo-eh
87	Us	Wareware ni	Wah-deh-wah-deh nee
88	Use (I use)	Tsukau	Tsoo-kah-oo
89	Very	Taihen	Tie-hehn
90	We	Watashitachi	Wah-tah-shee-tah-chee
91	What	Nani	Nah-nee
92	When	Itsu	Ee-tsoo
93	Where	Doko	Doh-koh
94	Which	Dore	Do're
95	Who	Donata	Do'nah'ta
96	Why	Naze	Nah'ze
97	With	De	Den
98	Yes	Hai	Hie
99	You	Anata	Ah-nah-tah
100	Your	Anata no	Ah-nah-tah noh

	English	Esperanto	Esperanto Pronunciation
1	A, an	–	–
2	After	Post	Post
3	Again	Denove	De-nor've
4	All	Tuto	Too'tor
5	Almost	Preskau	Pres'kow
6	Also	Ankau	Ahn'kow
7	Always	Ciam	Chee'um
8	And	Kaj	K'eye
9	Because	Car	Churr
10	Before	Antau	Anh'tow
11	Big	Granda	Grun'dah
12	But	Sed	Sed
13	Can (I can)	Mi povas	Mee por'vus
14	Come (I Come)	Mi venas	Mee ven'us
15	Either/or	Au/au	Ow ow
16	Find (I find)	Mi trovas	Mee tror'vus
17	First	Unua	Oo-noo'ah
18	For	Por	Porr
19	Friend	Amiko	Ah-mee'kor
20	From	De	Deh
21	Go (I go)	Mi iras	Mee eer'us

	English	*Esperanto*	*Esperanto Pronunciation*
22	Good	Bona	Bor nah
23	Goodbye	Gis la revido	Jeess lah re-vee'dor
24	Happy	Felica	Fell-eetch'ah
25	Have (I have)	Mi havas	Mee hah'vus
26	He	Li	Lee
27	Hello	Saluton	Sul-oo'ton
28	Here	Tie ci	Tee'eh chee
29	How	Kiel	Kee-el
30	I	Me	Mee
31	I am	Mi estas	Mee ess'tus
32	If	Se	Seh
33	In	En	Enn
34	Know (I know)	Mi scias	Mee stsee'us
35	Last	Lasta	Luss'tah
36	Like (I like)	Mi satas	Mee shah'tus
37	Little	Malgranda	Mul-grun'dah
38	Love (I love)	Mi amas	Mee ahm'us
39	Make (I make)	Mi faras	Mee fah'rus
40	Many	Multaj	Mool-t'eye
41	Me	Min	Meen
42	More	Pli	Plee
43	Most	Plej	Play
44	Much	Multo	Mool'tor
45	My	Mia	Mee'ah
46	New	Nova	Nor'vah
47	No	Ne	Neh
48	Not	Ne	Neh
49	Now	Nun	Noon
50	Of	De	Deh
51	Often	Ofte	Offt'ay
52	On	Sur	Soor
53	One	Unu	Oo'noo
54	Only	Nur	Noor
55	Or	Au	Ow
56	Other	Alia	Ul-ee'ah
57	Our	Nia	Nee'ah
58	Out	El	El
59	Over	Super	Soo'payr
60	People	Homoj	Hor'moy
61	Place	Loko	Lor'kor
62	Please	Bonvolu	Bon-vor'loo
63	Same	Sama	Sah'mah
64	See (I see)	Mi vidas	Mee vee'dus

	English	*Esperanto*	*Esperanto Pronunciation*
65	She	Si	She
66	So	Tiel	Tee'el
67	Some	Kelkaj	Kel'kay
68	Sometimes	Kelkfoje	Kelk-foy'ay
69	Still	Ankorau	Unk-or-ow
70	Such	Tiel	Tee'el
71	Tell (I tell)	Mi diras	Mee dee'rus
72	Thank you	Dankon	Dun'kon
73	That	Ke	Kay
74	The	La	Lah
75	Their	Ilia	Ill-ee'ah
76	Them	Ilin	Ill'een
77	Then	Tiam	Tee'um
78	There is, There are	Jen	Yen
79	They	Ili	Ee'lee
80	Thing	Ajo	Ah'zho
81	Think (I think)	Mi pensas	Mee pen'sus
82	This	Tiu ci	Tee'oo chee
83	Time	Tempo	Tem'por
84	To	Al	Ull
85	Under	Sub	Soob
86	Up	Supren	Soop'ren
87	Us	Nin	Neen
88	Use (I use)	Mi uzas	Mee ooz'us
89	Very	Tre	Tray
90	We	Ni	Nee
91	What	Kio	Kee'or
92	When	Kiam	Kee'm
93	Where	Kie	Kee'ay
94	Which	Kio	Kee'oh
95	Who	Kiu	Kee'oo
96	Why	Kial	Kee'arl
97	With	Kun	Koon
98	Yes	Jes	Yes
99	You	Vi	Vee
100	Your	Via	Vee'ah

CHAPTER ELEVEN

COUNTRIES/CAPITALS

If you regularly watch or listen to the news, or subscribe to a daily newspaper, then you will be 'confronted' with the countries and capitals of the world on an almost daily basis. Despite this regular 'familiarity' with the information, most people can name no more than ten countries with their appropriate capital, and have very little idea of where each country is.

The reason for this is once again the negative spiral, in which the more you know you don't know, the more rapidly your mind becomes confused with the bombardment of new information, the less is learnt, and the more even what you *do* know becomes eventually confused.

By memorising each country and its capital, and by mentally imagining the country's location with the aid of the map on pages 160 and 161, you will find that the more you see, hear and read about the countries and the capitals, the more you will increasingly know and remember.

In a period of less than a year you will have a knowledge of the location of the countries and capitals of the world, and of the current events that relate to them, that will rank you, literally and mathematically, as one in a million!

	Country	***Capital***
1	Afghanistan	Kabul
2	Albania	Tirane
3	Algeria	Algiers
4	Andorra	Andorra
5	Angola	Luanda
6	Antigua & Barbuda	St John's
7	Argentina	Buenos Aires
8	Australia	Canberra
9	Austria	Vienna
10	Bahamas	Nassau
11	Bahrain	Manama

	Country	*Capital*
12	Bangladesh	Dhaka
13	Barbados	Bridgetown
14	Belgium	Brussels
15	Belize	Belmopan
16	Benin	Porto Novo
17	Bhutan	Thimphu
18	Bolivia	La Paz
19	Botswana	Gaborone
20	Brazil	Brasilia
21	Brunei	Bandar Seri Begawan
22	Bulgaria	Sofia
23	Burkina Faso	Ouagadougou
24	Burma	Rangoon
25	Burundi	Bujumbura
26	Cambodia (Kampuchea)	Phnom Penh
27	Cameroon	Yaounde
28	Canada	Ottawa
29	Cape Verde	Praia
30	Central African Republic	Bangui
31	Chad	N'djamena
32	Chile	Santiago
33	China	Beijing
34	Colombia	Bogota
35	Comoros	Moroni
36	Congo	Brazzaville
37	Costa Rica	San Jose
38	Cuba	Havana
39	Cyprus	Nicosia
40	Czechoslovakia	Prague
41	Denmark	Copenhagen
42	Djibouti	Djibouti
43	Dominica	Roseau
44	Dominican Republic	Santo Domingo
45	East Germany	Berlin
46	Ecuador	Quito
47	Egypt	Cairo
48	El Salvador	San Salvador
49	Equatorial Guinea	Malabo
50	Ethiopia	Addis Ababa
51	Falkland Islands	Stanley
52	Fiji	Suva
53	Finland	Helsinki
54	France	Paris
55	French Guiana	Cayenne

	Country	*Capital*
56	Gabon	Libreville
57	Gambia	Banjul
58	Ghana	Accra
59	Greece	Athens
60	Grenada	St George's
61	Guatemala	Guatemala
62	Guinea	Conakry
63	Guinea-Bissau	Bissau
64	Guyana	Georgetown
65	Haiti	Port au Prince
66	Honduras	Tegucigalpa
67	Hungary	Budapest
68	Iceland	Reykjavik
69	India	New Delhi
70	Indonesia	Java
71	Iran	Tehran
72	Iraq	Baghdad
73	Ireland	Dublin
74	Israel	Jerusalem
75	Italy	Rome
76	Ivory Coast	Abidjan
77	Jamaica	Kingston
78	Japan	Tokyo
79	Jordan	Amman
80	Kenya	Nairobi
81	Kiribate	Agana
82	Kuwait	Kuwait
83	Laos	Vientiane
84	Lebanon	Beirut
85	Lesotho	Maseru
86	Liberia	Monrovia
87	Libya	Tripoli
88	Liechtenstein	Vaduz
89	Luxembourg	Luxembourg
90	Madagascar	Antananarivo
91	Malawi	Lilongwe
92	Malaysia	Kuala Lumpur
93	Maldives	Male
94	Mali	Bamako
95	Malta	Valleta
96	Mauritania	Nouakchott
97	Mauritius	Port Louis
98	Mexico	Mexico City
99	Monaco	Monaco

	Country	*Capital*
100	Mongolia	Ulaanbaatar
101	Morocco	Rabat
102	Mozambique	Maputo
103	Namibia	Windhoek
104	Nepal	Katmandu
105	Netherlands	Amsterdam
106	New Zealand	Wellington
107	Nicaragua	Managua
108	Niger	Niamey
109	Nigeria	Lagos
110	North Korea	Pyongyang
111	Norway	Oslo
112	Oman	Muscat
113	Pakistan	Islamabad
114	Panama	Panama
115	Papua New Guinea	Port Moresby
116	Paraguay	Asuncion
117	Peru	Lima
118	Philippines	Manila
119	Poland	Warsaw
120	Portugal	Lisbon
121	Puerto Rico	San Juan
122	Qatar	Doha
123	Romania	Bucharest
124	Rwanda	Kigali
125	St Kitt's & Nevis	Basseterre
126	St Lucia	Castries
127	St Vincent	Kingstown
128	Sao Tome & Principe	Sao Tome
129	Saudi Arabia	Riyadh
130	Senegal	Dakar
131	Seychelles	Victoria
132	Sierra Leone	Freetown
133	Singapore	Singapore
134	Solomon Islands	Honiara
135	Somalia	Mogadishu
136	South Africa	Pretoria
137	South Korea	Seoul
138	Soviet Union	Moscow
139	Spain	Madrid
140	Sri Lanka	Colombo
141	Sudan	Khartoum
142	Suriname	Paramaribo
143	Swaziland	Mbabane

	Country	*Capital*
144	Sweden	Stockholm
145	Switzerland	Bern
146	Syria	Damascus
147	Taiwan	Taipei
148	Tanzania	Dar es Salaam
149	Thailand	Bangkok
150	Tonga	Nukualofa
151	Togo	Lome
152	Trinidad & Tobago	Port of Spain
153	Tunisia	Tunis
154	Turkey	Ankara
155	Uganda	Kampala
156	United Arab Emirates	Abu Dhabi
157	United Kingdom	London
158	United States	Washington
159	Uruguay	Montevideo
160	Vanuatu	Vita
161	Venezuela	Caracas
162	Vietnam	Hanoi
163	West Germany	Bonn
164	Western Samoa	Apia
165	Yemen	San 'a
166	Yemen (P.D.R. of)	Aden
167	Yugoslavia	Belgrade
168	Zaire	Kinshasa
169	Zambia	Lusaka
170	Zimbabwe	Harare

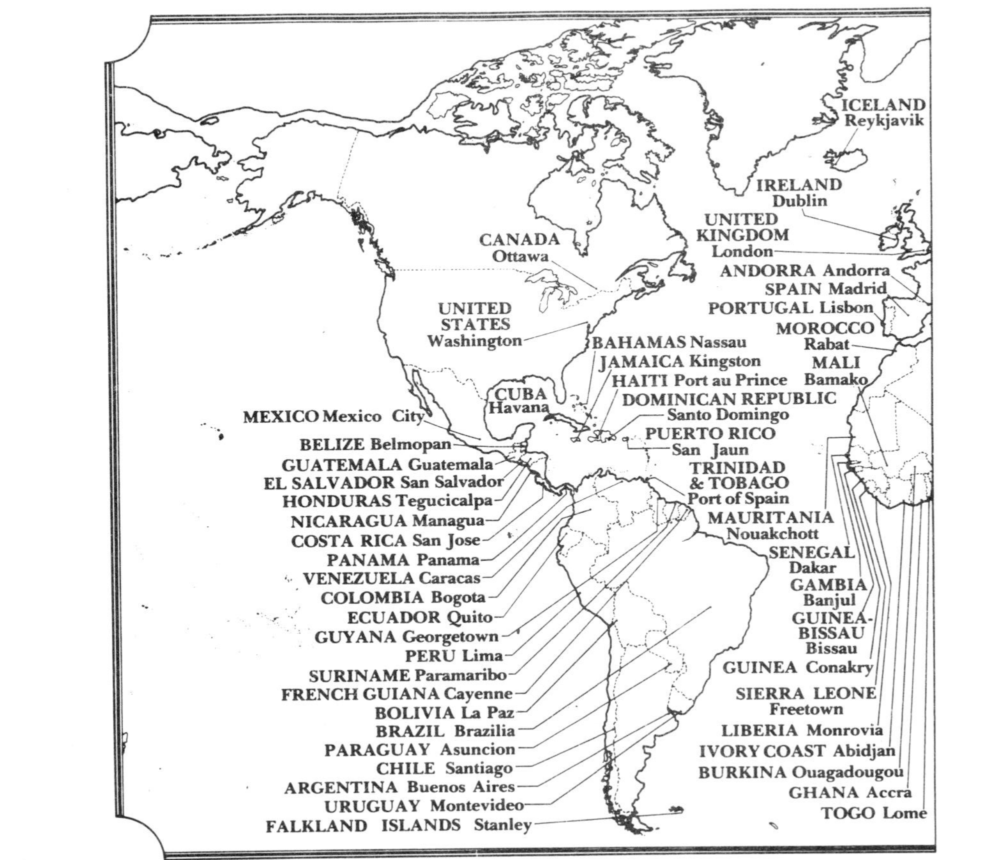
ICELAND Reykjavik
IRELAND Dublin
UNITED KINGDOM London
ANDORRA Andorra
SPAIN Madrid
PORTUGAL Lisbon
MOROCCO Rabat
MALI Bamako
CANADA Ottawa
UNITED STATES Washington
BAHAMAS Nassau
JAMAICA Kingston
HAITI Port au Prince
DOMINICAN REPUBLIC Santo Domingo
PUERTO RICO San Jaun
TRINIDAD & TOBAGO Port of Spain
CUBA Havana
MEXICO Mexico City
BELIZE Belmopan
GUATEMALA Guatemala
EL SALVADOR San Salvador
HONDURAS Tegucicalpa
NICARAGUA Managua
COSTA RICA San Jose
PANAMA Panama
VENEZUELA Caracas
COLOMBIA Bogota
ECUADOR Quito
GUYANA Georgetown
PERU Lima
SURINAME Paramaribo
FRENCH GUIANA Cayenne
BOLIVIA La Paz
BRAZIL Brazilia
PARAGUAY Asuncion
CHILE Santiago
ARGENTINA Buenos Aires
URUGUAY Montevideo
FALKLAND ISLANDS Stanley
MAURITANIA Nouakchott
SENEGAL Dakar
GAMBIA Banjul
GUINEA-BISSAU Bissau
GUINEA Conakry
SIERRA LEONE Freetown
LIBERIA Monrovia
IVORY COAST Abidjan
BURKINA Ouagadougou
GHANA Accra
TOGO Lome

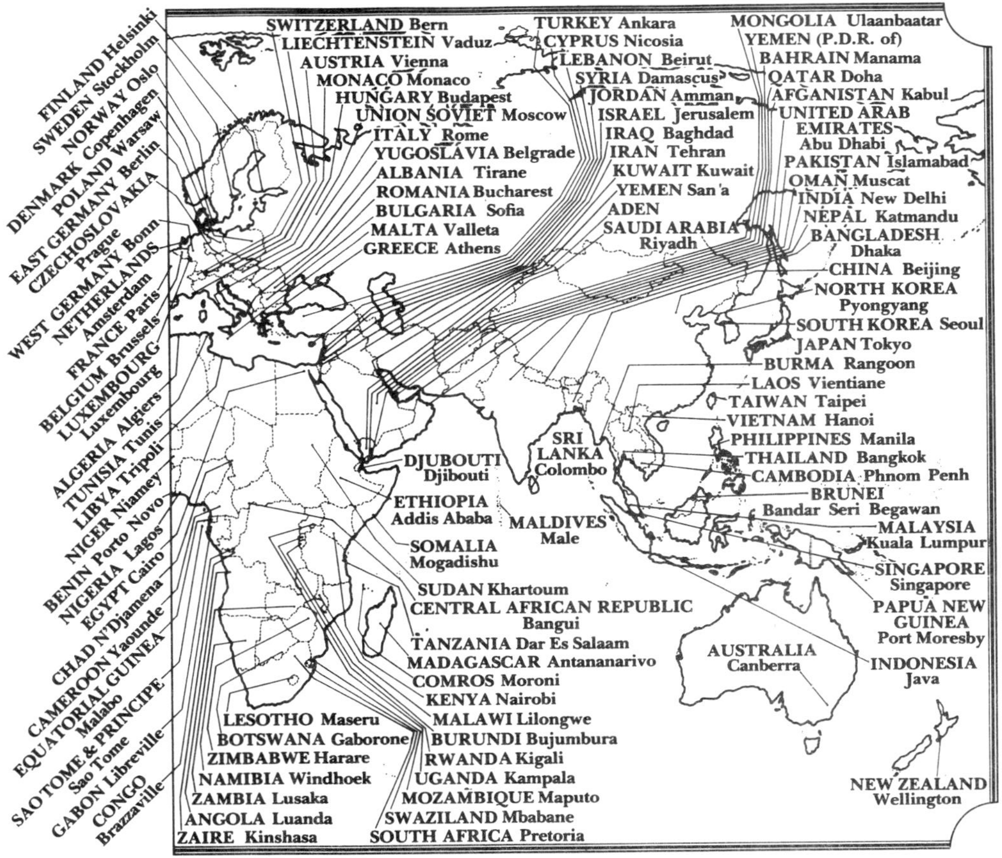

FINLAND Helsinki
SWEDEN Stockholm
NORWAY Oslo
DENMARK Copenhagen
POLAND Warsaw
EAST GERMANY Berlin
CZECHOSLOVAKIA Prague
WEST GERMANY Bonn
NETHERLANDS Amsterdam
FRANCE Paris
BELGIUM Brussels
LUXEMBOURG Luxembourg
ALGERIA Algiers
TUNISIA Tunis
LIBYA Tripoli
NIGER Niamey
BENIN Porto Novo
NIGERIA Lagos
EGYPT Cairo
CHAD N'Djamena
CAMEROON Yaounde
EQUATORIAL GUINEA Malabo
SAO TOME & PRINCIPE Sao Tome
GABON Libreville
CONGO Brazzaville

SWITZERLAND Bern
LIECHTENSTEIN Vaduz
AUSTRIA Vienna
MONACO Monaco
HUNGARY Budapest
UNION SOVIET Moscow
ITALY Rome
YUGOSLAVIA Belgrade
ALBANIA Tirane
ROMANIA Bucharest
BULGARIA Sofia
MALTA Valleta
GREECE Athens

TURKEY Ankara
CYPRUS Nicosia
LEBANON Beirut
SYRIA Damascus
JORDAN Amman
ISRAEL Jerusalem
IRAQ Baghdad
IRAN Tehran
KUWAIT Kuwait
YEMEN San'a
ADEN
SAUDI ARABIA Riyadh

MONGOLIA Ulaanbaatar
YEMEN (P.D.R. of)
BAHRAIN Manama
QATAR Doha
AFGANISTAN Kabul
UNITED ARAB EMIRATES Abu Dhabi
PAKISTAN Islamabad
OMAN Muscat
INDIA New Delhi
NEPAL Katmandu
BANGLADESH Dhaka
CHINA Beijing
NORTH KOREA Pyongyang
SOUTH KOREA Seoul
JAPAN Tokyo
BURMA Rangoon
LAOS Vientiane
TAIWAN Taipei
VIETNAM Hanoi
PHILIPPINES Manila
THAILAND Bangkok
CAMBODIA Phnom Penh
BRUNEI Bandar Seri Begawan
MALAYSIA Kuala Lumpur
SINGAPORE Singapore
PAPUA NEW GUINEA Port Moresby
INDONESIA Java
AUSTRALIA Canberra
NEW ZEALAND Wellington

SRI LANKA Colombo
MALDIVES Male
DJUBOUTI Djibouti
ETHIOPIA Addis Ababa
SOMALIA Mogadishu
SUDAN Khartoum
CENTRAL AFRICAN REPUBLIC Bangui
TANZANIA Dar Es Salaam
MADAGASCAR Antananarivo
COMROS Moroni
KENYA Nairobi
MALAWI Lilongwe
BURUNDI Bujumbura
RWANDA Kigali
UGANDA Kampala
MOZAMBIQUE Maputo
SWAZILAND Mbabane
SOUTH AFRICA Pretoria

LESOTHO Maseru
BOTSWANA Gaborone
ZIMBABWE Harare
NAMIBIA Windhoek
ZAMBIA Lusaka
ANGOLA Luanda
ZAIRE Kinshasa

CHAPTER TWELVE

KINGS AND QUEENS OF ENGLAND

For those who are in any way interested in the history of England, the knowledge of the time-location and duration of reign provides an excellent matrix on which to 'hang' other knowledge matrices, including social, literary, religious, musical, artistic and scientific.

By this stage your skill with SEM^3 should have reached such a level that memorising this entire chunk of history, (a task considered practically impossible by most history students) will take less than an hour!

		from	*to*
1	William I	1066	1087
2	William II	1087	1100
3	Henry I	1100	1135
4	Stephen	1135	1154
5	Henry II	1154	1189
6	Richard I	1189	1199
7	John	1199	1216
8	Henry III	1216	1272
9	Edward I	1272	1307
10	Edward II	1307	1327
11	Edward III	1327	1377
12	Richard II	1377	1399
13	Henry IV	1399	1413
14	Henry V	1413	1422
15	Henry VI	1422	1461
16	Edward IV	1461	1483
17	Edward V	1483	1483
18	Richard III	1483	1485
19	Henry VII	1485	1509
20	Henry VIII	1509	1547
21	Edward VI	1547	1553
22	Jane	1553	1553
23	Mary I	1553	1558
24	Elizabeth I	1558	1603
25	James I	1603	1625
26	Charles I	1625	1649
27	Oliver Cromwell: Lord Protector	1653	1658
28	Richard Cromwell: Lord Protector	1658	1659
29	Charles II	1660	1685
30	James II	1685	1688
31	William III and	1688	1702
32	Mary II	1688	1694
33	Anne	1702	1714
34	George I	1714	1727
35	George II	1727	1760
36	George III	1760	1820
37	George IV	1820	1830
38	William IV	1830	1837
39	Victoria	1837	1901
40	Edward VII	1901	1910
41	George V	1910	1936
42	Edward VIII	1936	1936
43	George VI	1936	1952
44	Elizabeth II	1952	

CHAPTER THIRTEEN

THE HUMAN BODY – MUSCULATURE

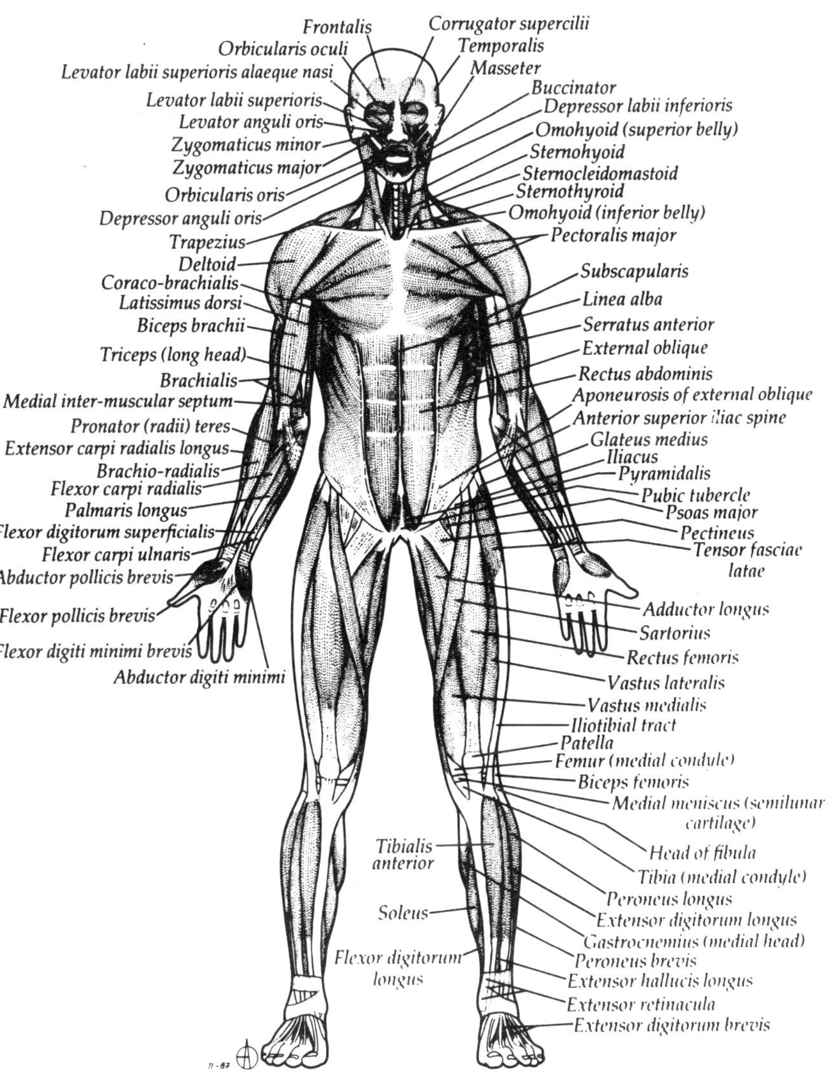

Memorising your own musculature gives you a more accurate understanding and appreciation of your own extraordinary complexity, allows you to train yourself with more precision and delicacy, to react more appropriately to any injury or medical condition, and to appreciate even more the accomplishments of those who have trained their own musculature to the level of championship performance.

Mental giants such as Michelangelo and Leonardo da Vinci spent years of their lives investigating the body's intricate interconnections and biophysical mechanics.

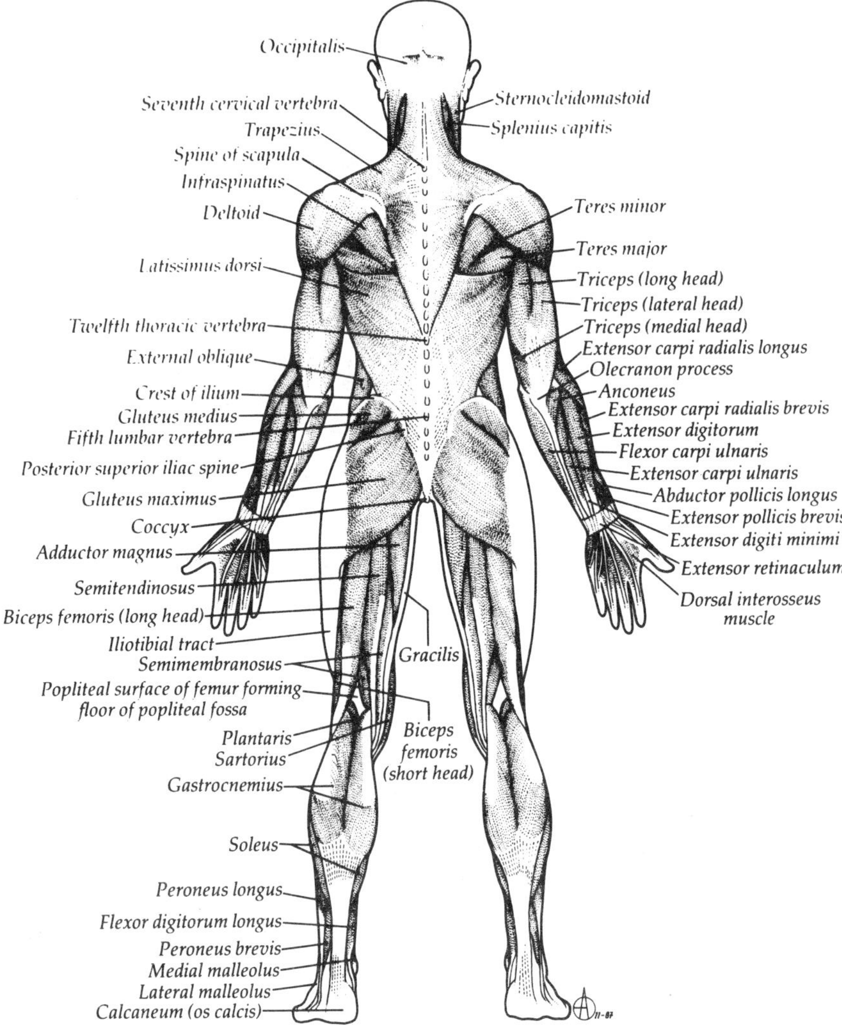

CHAPTER FOURTEEN

THE ELEMENTS

Our selves, our planet, our solar system and indeed our universe are made up primarily of 105 elements or 'basic working parts'.

Thus the vast majesty of the microcosmous and macrocosmous that surrounds us can, like a language, have its astounding complexity reduced to fundamental operating parts that allow us to understand and learn about it with much greater facility.

Once you have control of these, and the way in which they fit together, your ability to create understanding and inter-relationships and 'structures' within the field becomes limitless.

Using SEM^3 you will be able to lay a complete foundation for your growing understanding of the physical, chemical and biological worlds around you – a level of understanding that most never retain, even after four years of study.

You will also be laying the cornerstones for answering those probing questions that the brains of children ask in order for them to understand the world around them: 'Why does water go hard when it's cold?'; 'Why do things smell and taste different?'; 'Why do sugar and salt taste different although they look the same?'; 'Why do I have to eat?!'

As SEM^3 is a Master Matrix that allows you to structure your memory, so the Matrix of the chemical elements is a Master Matrix that allows you to understand and structure the nature of the physical universe.

The names of the various families or groupings of the elements are abbreviations of the following:

Hydrogen	Hydrogen
Noble Gases	Noble Gases
Alkaline	Alkali and Alkaline Earth Metals
Boron/Carbon	Boron and Carbon Families
Nitrogen/Oxygen	Nitrogen and Oxygen Families
The Halogens	The Halogens
Early Trans Metals	Early Transition Metals
Late Trans Metals	Late Transition Metals
The Triads	The Triads
Rare Earth Metals	Rare Earth Metals
Actinide	Actinide Metals

Atomic Number *Element* *Symbol* *Atomic Weight* *Family*

1 HYDROGEN H 1.008 HYDROGEN
From hydor and gen, or water-forming; discovered in 1766; third most abundant and lightest element. Hydrogen is almost never found free on earth, but the sun and other stars are almost pure hydrogen. The thermonuclear fusion of hydrogen nuclei lights and heats the universe.

2 HELIUM He 4.0026 NOBLE GASES
From helios, or sun; discovered in 1868; almost all the helium in the world comes from natural gas wells in the United States. One well in Arizona produces a gas that is 8% helium. Lighter than air, it is widely used in balloons in place of highly inflammable hydrogen.

3 LITHIUM Li 6.941 ALKALINE
From lithos, discovered in 1817; the lightest of the solid elements. Lithium forms a black oxide when exposed to air. It is used in ceramics, alloys, in the H-bomb – and in treating both gout victims and manic-depressives.

4 BERYLLIUM Be 9.012 ALKALINE
From the mineral beryl, in which it was found in 1798. This element produces alloys that are extremely elastic, hence its role in making gears, springs and other machine parts. Because of its high melting point – 1,285°C – beryllium goes into making rocket nose cones.

5 BORON B 10.811 BORON/CARBON
From borax and carbon; discovered 1808. A non-metal, boron is best known in borax (sodium borate) and in boric-acid – the one acid that is good for the eyes. About a million tons of boron are used in industry each year. In agriculture it serves as both a plant food and a weed killer.

6 CARBON C 12.011 BORON/CARBON
From carbo, or charcoal; prehistoric. Carbon, in its endless variety of compounds, is an indispensable source of everyday products, such as nylon and petrol, perfume and plastics, shoe polish, DDT and TNT.

7 NITROGEN N 14.007 NITROGEN/OXYGEN
From nitron and gen, or nitre-forming; discovered in 1772; a gas making up 78% of the air. Nitrogen can be 'fixed' from the air – compounds include the anaesthetic 'laughing gas', explosives such as TNT, fertilisers, and amino-acids – the building blocks of protein.

Atomic Number	*Element*	*Symbol*	*Atomic Weight*	*Family*
8	OXYGEN	O	15.999	NITROGEN/OXYGEN

From oxys and gen, or acid-forming; discovered in 1774; the most abundant element, making up about half of everything on earth, 21% of the atmosphere by volume and two-thirds of the human body. Breathed in by animals, oxygen is restored to the air by plants.

9	FLOURINE	F	18.998	HALOGENS

From flou, or flow; discovered in 1771. Fluorine is the most reactive of the non-metals; only a few of the inert gases resist it. It corrodes platinum, a material that withstands most other chemicals. In a stream of flourine gas, wood and rubber burst into flame – and even asbestos glows.

10	NEON	Ne	20.183	NOBLE GASES

From neos, or new; discovered 1898. The best known of the inert gases, it is chiefly used in advertising. The ubiquitous 'neon sign' is a glass vacuum tube containing a minute amount of neon gas; when an electric current is passed through, the tube gives off a bright orange-red light.

11	SODIUM	Na	22.990	ALKALINE

From soda; symbol from its Latin name Natrium; discovered 1807; sixth most abundant element. Metallic sodium is too violent for most everyday uses and is generally stored in paraffin. But its useful compounds include table salt, baking soda, borax and lye.

12	MAGNESIUM	Mg	24.3	ALKALINE

From Magnesia, an ancient city in Asia Minor; discovered 1775; eighth most abundant element; burns as a powder or foil in fire-crackers, bombs, and flash bulbs. It has one odd biological effect: a deficiency in man can have the same effect as alcoholism, delirium tremens.

13	ALUMINIUM	Al	26.982	BORON/CARBON

From alumen, or alum; discovered 1827; the most abundant metal and third most abundant element, its uses range from toothpaste tubes to aeroplane wings. Early samples cost £230 per pound; now over a million tons are produced yearly in the U.S. for as low as £0.30 per pound.

14	SILICON	Si	28.086	BORON/CARBON

From silex, or flint; discovered 1823; the second most abundant element – making up one-quarter of the earth's crust. Sand, largely silicon dioxide, goes into making glass and cement. Pure silicon is used in micro-electronic devices such as solar batteries to power satellite instruments.

Atomic Number	*Element*	*Symbol*	*Atomic Weight*	*Family*
15	PHOSPHORUS	P	30.974	NITROGEN/OXYGEN

From phosphoros, or light bearer; discovered 1669; occurs in three major forms – white, red and rarely black. The white so unstable that it yellows then reddens in light, glows in the dark – hence 'phosphorescence'. Phosphates are ingredients of detergents.

16	SULPHUR	S	32.064	NITROGEN/OXYGEN

From sulphur, or brimstone its biblical name; recognised since ancient times. Used in all branches of modern industry, it turns up among other places in matches, insecticides and rubber tyres. Nearly 200 pounds of sulphuric acid per capita are produced in the U.S. each year.

17	CHLORINE	Cl	35.453	HALOGENS

From chloros, or greenish-yellow; discovered 1774. Combining with almost as many elements as florine, chlorine is less corrosive but strong enough to be used as a bleach, a disinfectant and a poison gas. Pure chlorine is commonly prepared from ordinary salt.

18	ARGON	Ar	39.948	NOBLE GASES

From argon, or inactive; discovered 1894. The most abundant of noble gases, argon makes up 0.934% of the air. Its industrial forte is in welding; it provides an inert atmosphere in which welded metals will not burn. It is also the gas that fills ordinary incandescent light bulbs.

19	POTASSIUM	K	39.1	ALKALINE

From potash, an impure form of potassium carbonate known to the ancients; symbol K from its Latin name kalium; discovered 1807. Seventh most abundant element in the earth's crust. Its radioactivity, though mild, may be one natural cause of genetic mutation in man.

20	CALCIUM	Ca	40.08	ALKALINE

From calx, or lime – an oxide of calcium; discovered 1808; fifth most abundant in the earth's crust. Its presence in our bodies is essential. Normal quota in an adult is about 2 pounds, mostly in the teeth and bones. Calcium also plays a role in regulating the heartbeat.

21	SCANDIUM	Sc	44.956	EARLY TRANS METALS

From Scandinavia; discovered 1879. Although no practical uses have yet been found for this metal, its potential is great because it is almost as light as aluminium and has a much higher melting point. A pound of scandium produced in 1960 was the first such quantity made.

Atomic Number	*Element*	*Symbol*	*Atomic Weight*	*Family*
22	TITANIUM	Ti	47.9	EARLY TRANS METALS

From Titans, the supermen of Greek myth; discovered in 1791. Although it is the ninth most abundant element, titanium has only begun to serve man. Its white dioxide goes into bright paints. The metal itself is used in constructing supersonic aircraft such as Concorde.

23	VANADIUM	V	50.942	EARLY TRANS METALS

From Vanadis, a Scandinavian goddess; discovered 1830. Added to steel, vanadium produces one of the toughest alloys for armour plate, axles, piston rods and crankshafts. Less than 1% of vanadium and a little chromium makes steel shock and vibration resistant.

24	CHROMIUM	Cr	51.996	EARLY TRANS METALS

From chroma, or colour; discovered 1797. A very bright silvery metal, it forms compounds valued as pigments for their vivid green, yellow, red and orange colours. The ruby takes its colour from chromium. Besides lustrous chrome plate, its alloys include a number of special hard steels.

25	MANGANESE	Mn	54.938	EARLY TRANS METALS

From magnes, or magnet – its ore was first confused with magnetic iron ore; discovered 1774. Manganese which gives steel a hard yet pliant quality, seems to play a similar role in animal bone: without it, bones grow spongier and break more easily. It activates many enzymes.

26	IRON	Fe	55.847	TRIADS

From iren, its old English name; symbol Fe from its Latin name, ferrum; first utilised by prehistoric man. The fourth most abundant element and the cheapest metal, iron is the basic ingredient of all steel. Making up part of the compound haemoglobin, it carries oxygen in the blood stream.

27	COBALT	Co	58.933	TRIADS

From kobold, or evil spirit (its poisonous ores were once treacherous to mine); discovered 1735. For centuries cobalt's blue salts have given colour to porcelains, tiles and enamels. Its alloys go into making jet propulsion engines, and its radioactive isotope is used to treat cancer.

28	NICKEL	Ni	58.7	TRIADS

From the German Kupfernickel, or false copper, a reddish ore contains nickel but no copper; discovered 1751. Its hard durable qualities have long made nickel popular for coins – the U.S. 5 cent piece is 25% nickel, the rest copper. Nickel plate protects softer metals.

Atomic Number	*Element*	*Symbol*	*Atomic Weight*	*Family*
29	COPPER	Cu	63.5	LATE TRANS METALS

From cuprum, derived from the ancient name of Cyprus, famed for its copper mines; known by early man. It and gold are the only two coloured metals. Alloyed in most gold jewellery and silverware, copper is mixed with zinc in brass, with tin in bronze. A 'copper' penny is bronze.

30	ZINC	Zn	65.38	LATE TRANS METALS

Probably from zin, German for tin; discovered by the alchemist Paracelsus in 16th century, though the zinc-copper alloy brass was known to the ancients. While not technically a coloured metal, zinc has a bluish cast. An excellent coating metal, it is used to line flashlight batteries.

31	GALLIUM	Ga	69.72	BORON/CARBON

From Gallia, the old name for France; discovered 1875. A metal that melts in the hand, it is one of the few that expands as it freezes, as do non-metals and most gases. Its high boiling point – 1,983°C – makes it ideal for recording temperatures that would vaporise a thermometer.

32	GERMANIUM	Ge	72.59	BORON/CARBON

From Germany; discovered 1886. The first metal in the carbon family, germanium resembles the non-metal silicon. The first element used for transistors, it has brought about the replacement of large vacuum tubes with devices 1/400″ across.

33	ARSENIC	As	74.933	NITROGEN/OXYGEN

From arsenikos, or male (the Greeks believed metals differed in sex); discovered about 1250. Best classed as a non-metal with a few metallic traits, arsenic is famed as a poison but some of its compounds are medicines. When heated it 'sublimes' – i.e. the solid evaporises directly.

34	SELENIUM	Se	78.96	NITROGEN/OXYGEN

From selene, or moon; discovered 1817; exists both as metal and non-metal. Unlike most electrical conductors, selenium varies in conductivity with variations in light. This 'photo-electric' trait suits it for service in electric eyes, solar cells, television cameras and light meters.

35	BROMINE	Br	79.9	HALOGENS

From bromos, or stench; discovered 1826; a red, caustic, fuming liquid, with a foul smell. Bromine is an effective disinfectant. Among its compounds are the bromides, used in nerve sedatives, and in petrol anti-knock compounds that make car engines run smoothly.

Atomic Number ***Element*** ***Symbol*** ***Atomic Weight*** ***Family***

36 KRYPTON Kr 83.8 NOBLE GASES

From kryptos, or hidden; discovered in 1898. Radioactive krypton is used to keep tabs on Soviet nuclear production. Because this gas is a by-product of all nuclear reactors, the Russian share is found by subtracting the amount that comes from Western reactors from the total in the air.

37 RUBIDIUM Rb 85.47 ALKALINE

From rubidus, or red (the colour its salts impart to flames); discovered 1861. Used in electric eye-cells, also a potential space fuel. Like potassium, it is slightly radioactive, and has been used to locate brain tumours, as it collects in tumours but not in normal tissue.

38 STRONTIUM Sr 87.62 ALKALINE

From Strontian, Scotland; discovered 1790; a rare metal which is a sort of evil alter ego of life-supporting calcium. Radioactive strontium 90 is present in atomic fall-out. It is absorbed by bone tissue in place of calcium, and enough of it destroys marrow and can cause cancer.

39 YTTRIUM Y 88.9 EARLY TRANS METALS

From the town of Ytterby, Sweden, where it was discovered in 1794; a scaly metal with an iron-grey sheen. Yttrium 90, a radioactive isotope, has a dramatic medical use in needles which have replaced the surgeon's knife in killing pain-transmitting nerves in the spinal cord.

40 ZIRCONIUM Zr 91.22 EARLY TRANS METALS

From zircon, the name of the semiprecious gemstone in which it was discovered in 1789. A metal unaffected by neutrons, zirconium serves as the inner lining of reactors in nuclear submarines and atomic power plants. It is also used as a building material for jets and rockets.

41 NIOBIUM Nb 92.906 EARLY TRANS METALS

From Niobe, daughter of the mythical Greek king Tantalus (niobium is found with tantalum); discovered 1801. Used in steel, atomic reactors, jet engines and rockets, it was known until 1950 as colombium, from Columbus – a poetic name for America, where its ore was first discovered.

42 MOLYBDENUM Mo 95.94 EARLY TRANS METALS

From molybdos, or lead – first found in what was first thought to be lead-ore; discovered 1778. Fifth highest melting metal, it is used in boiler plate, rifle barrels and filaments. No vessel could be found in which to cast it until a special water-cooled crucible was devised in 1959.

Atomic Number	*Element*	*Symbol*	*Atomic Weight*	*Family*
43	TECHNETIUM	Tc	98	EARLY TRANS METALS

From technetos, or artificial; produced 1937. The first man-made element, it was originally produced by the atomic bombardment of molybdenum. Later it was found among the fission products of uranium.

44	RUTHENIUM	Ru	101.07	THE TRIADS

From Ruthenia, Latin for Russia; discovered 1844. Pure ruthenium is too hard and brittle to machine. It makes a top-notch 'hardener', however, when it is alloyed with platinum. But used in excess of 15%, ruthemium is ruinous, making the metals too hard to be worked.

45	RHODIUM	Rh	102.91	THE TRIADS

From rhodon, or rose (its salts give a rosy solution); discovered 1803. Besides forming alloys, rhodium makes a lustrous, hard coating for other metals in such items as table silver and camera parts. A thin film of vaporized rhodium deposited on glass makes excellent mirrors.

46	PALLADIUM	Pd	106.4	THE TRIADS

After the asteroid Pallas; discovered 1803. Free from tarnish and corrosion-resistant, palladium is incorporated in contacts for telephone relays and high-grade surgical instruments. It is also used with gold, silver and other metals as a 'stiffener' in dental inlays and bridgework.

47	SILVER	Ag	107.87	LATE TRANS METALS

From Old English seolfor, for silver; symbol Ag from its Latin name argentum; prehistoric; the best conductor of heat and electricity. Its salts are basic in photography; when silver bromide is exposed to light, it undergoes a chemical change which the developer then makes visible.

48	CADMIUM	Cd	112.4	LATE TRANS METALS

From kadmia, or earth; discovered 1817. Cadmium occurs in nature with zinc. It makes excellent neutron-eating rods to slow up atomic chain reactions and finds use in nickel-cadmium batteries. Its bright sulphide makes the artist's popular pigment, cadmium yellow.

49	INDIUM	In	114.82	BORON/CARBON

From the indigo blue it shows in a spectroscope; discovered 1863. A metal used in engine bearings, in transistors and as a 'glue' that adheres to glass, it is too scarce for large-scale use. But a minuscule, long-lived indium battery has been devised to power new electronic wrist watches.

Atomic Number	*Element*	*Symbol*	*Atomic Weight*	*Family*

50 TIN Sn 118.69 BORON/CARBON

An Old English word; symbol Sn from stannum, Latin for tin. Prehistoric. Because it does not rust and resists other corrosion, tin has made possible the housewife's delight, canned food. A tin can is steel coated with about 0.0005 of an inch of tin. Over 40,000 million cans are made each year.

51 ANTIMONY Sb 121.75 NITROGEN/OXYGEN

From antimonas, 'opposed to solitude' (it generally occurs mixed with other elements); symbol Sb from stibium, or mark (it was once used as eyebrow pencil). Discovered about 1450. Antimony is mixed with lead in batteries and goes into type metal and pewter alloys.

52 TELLURIUM Te 127.60 NITROGEN/OXYGEN

From tellus, the earth; discovered 1782. With both metallic and non-metallic traits, tellurium has several peculiarities. It is 'out of step' in the periodic table, having a lower atomic number but higher atomic weight than iodine. And inhaling its vapour results in garlicky breath.

53 IODINE I 126.90 THE HALOGENS

From iodes, or violet; discovered 1811. A blue-black solid which turns into a violet vapour when heated. Formerly prepared from seaweed, it is now produced from oil-well brines. Most table salt is now 'iodised' to supplement the human diet; an iodine deficiency causes thyroid trouble.

54 XENON Xe 131.3 NOBLE GASES

From xenos, or stranger; discovered 1898. The rarest gas in the atmosphere, xenon is used in specialised light sources such as the high-speed electronic flash bulbs used by photographers. In these, the high volatility of its electron structure produces an instant, intense light.

55 CAESIUM Cs 132.91 ALKALINE

From caesius, or sky-blue (its salts turn flames blue); discovered 1860; the softest metal, liquid at warm room temperature, 28°C. Extremely reactive, it finds limited use in vacuum tubes and in atomic clocks so accurate that they vary no more than five seconds in ten generations.

56 BARIUM Ba 137.3 ALKALINE

From barys, hevy or dense; discovered 1808. The white sulphate is drunk as a medical cocktail to outline the stomach and intestines for X-ray examination. Barium nitrate gives fireworks a green colour.

Atomic Number	*Element*	*Symbol*	*Atomic Weight*	*Family*
57	LANTHANUM	La	138.91	EARLY TRANS METALS

From lanthanein, to lie hidden; discovered 1839; highly reactive. Because it gives glass special light-bending, or 'refractive', properties, lanthanum is used in expensive camera lenses. Radioactive lanthanum has been tested for use in treating cancer.

58	CERIUM	Ce	140.12	RARE EARTH METALS

After the asteroid Ceres; discovered 1803; most abundant of the rare-earth elements. It is the chief ingredient (just under 50%) of misch-metal alloy. Cerium is used in alloys to make heat-resistant jet-engines parts; its oxide is a promising new petroleum-cracking catalyst.

59	PRASEODYMIUM	Pr	140.91	RARE EARTH METALS

From prasios didymos, or green twin (from its green salts); discovered 1885 when separated from its rare-earth twin neodymium. Together they are now used in making lenses for glassmaker's goggles because they filter out the yellow light present in glass blowing.

60	NEODYMIUM	Nd	144.24	RARE EARTH METALS

From neos didymos, or new twin; discovered 1885. In a pure form, it produces the only bright-purple glass known. In a cruder state, it is used to take colour out of glass and to make special glass that transmits the tanning rays of the sun but not the unwanted infra-red heat rays.

61	PROMETHIUM	Pm	145	RARE EARTH METALS

After Prometheus; discovered 1947; the only rare earth that has never been found in nature. Produced in nuclear reactors, radioactive promethium in an 'atomic battery' no bigger than a drawing pin powers guided-missile instruments, watches and radios.

62	SAMARIUM	Sm	150.36	RARE EARTH METALS

From the mineral samarskite, named after a Russian mine official, Colonel V. E. Samarsky; discovered 1879. Calcium chloride crystals treated with samarium have been employed in lasers – devices for producing beams of light intense enough to burn metal or bounce off the moon.

63	EUROPIUM	Eu	151.96	RARE EARTH METALS

From Europe; discovered 1896. Most reactive rare earth. The metal had virtually no practical use until the atomic age. But atom for atom europium can absorb more neutrons than any other element, making it valuable in control rods for nuclear reactors.

Atomic Number	*Element*	*Symbol*	*Atomic Weight*	*Family*
64	GADOLINIUM	Gd	157.25	RARE EARTH METALS

From the mineral gadolinite, named after a Finnish chemist; discovered 1880. Falling in the middle of the rare-earth series, gadolinium divides the lighter metals, which tend to impart pliant qualities to alloys, from the heavier metals, used mostly as strengthening agents.

65	TERBIUM	Tb	158.9	RARE EARTH METALS

From Ytterby, Sweden; discovered 1843; named after the town that also gave its name to three other elements; the rare earths ytterbium and erbium and the transition metal yttrium. Like all rare earths, terbium in an impure state is pyrophoric – i.e. it bursts into flame when heated.

66	DYSPROSIUM	Dy	162.50	RARE EARTH METALS

From dysprositos, or hard to get at; discovered 1886. Dysprosium's chief practical use is in nuclear reactors, where it serves as a nuclear 'poison' – i.e. it is employed as a neutron-eating material to keep the neutron-spawning atomic chain reaction from getting out of hand.

67	HOLIUM	Ho	164.93	RARE EARTH METALS

From Holmia, Latin name for Stockholm; discovered 1879. Like dysprosium, holmium is a metal which can absorb fission-bred neutrons. It is used in nuclear reactors as a burnable poison – i.e. one that burns up while it is keeping a chain reaction from running out of control.

68	ERBIUM	Er	167.26	RARE EARTH METALS

From Ytterby, Sweden; discovered 1843. Used in ceramics as erbium oxide to produce a pink glaze. Erbium, holmium and dysprosium are almost identical in terms of their chemical and physical properties. They vary from each other only by one electron in their third inner orbit.

69	THULIUM	Tm	168.93	RARE EARTH METALS

From Thule, or Northland; discovered 1879. When irradiated in a nuclear reactor, thulium produces an isotope that gives off X-rays. A 'button' of this isotope is used to make a lightweight, portable X-ray machine for medical use. The 'hot' thulium is replaced every few months.

70	YTTERBIUM	Yb	173.04	RARE EARTH METALS

From Ytterby, Sweden; discovered 1907. This element is still little more than a laboratory curiosity. Along with the other rare earths, it recently turned up in the USSR in a mineral called gagarinite after the first astronaut. Easily oxidized.

Atomic Number	*Element*	*Symbol*	*Atomic Weight*	*Family*
71	LUTETIUM	Lu	174.97	RARE EARTH METALS

From Lutetia, the ancient name for Paris; discovered 1907; heaviest of the rare earths. Although rare-earth alloys such as misch metal are relatively cheap, pure lutetium is highly expensive. With many of its chemical and physical properties unknown, it has no practical value.

72	HAFNIUM	Hf	178.49	EARLY TRANS METALS

From Hafnia, the Latin name for Copenhagen; discovered 1923. A 'wonder metal' of the atomic age, hafnium has a great appetite for neutrons. Thus it goes into neutron-absorbing reactor control rods which slow down nuclear chain reactions and also quench atomic 'fires'.

73	TANTALUM	Ta	180.95	EARLY TRANS METALS

From King Tantalus of Greek myth; discovered 1802. Almost impervious to corrosion, tantalum is vital in surgical repairs of the human body; it can replace bone (for example in skull plates); as foil or wire it connects torn nerves; as woven gauze it binds up abdominal muscles.

74	TUNGSTEN	W	183.85	EARLY TRANS METALS

From Swedish tung sten, or heavy stone; symbol W from its German name wolfram; discovered 1783. The highest melting of metals – at 3,410°C – tungsten in filaments withstands intense heat in light bulbs. New tungsten-tipped 'painless' dental drills spin at ultra-high speed.

75	RHENIUM	Re	186.2	EARLY TRANS METALS

From the Rhine provinces of Germany; discovered 1925. Rhenium is the ninth scarcest element and has the second highest melting point. It is used in 'thermocouples' (electric thermometers for measuring high temperatures) and in the contact points of electrical switches.

76	OSMIUM	Os	190.2	THE TRIADS

From osme, or odour; discovered 1804. A metal with a pungent smell, it is used to produce alloys of extreme hardness. Pen tips and 'lifetime' gramophone needles are 60% osmium. It is the densest metal known: a brick-sized chunk of osmium weighs about 56 pounds.

77	IRIDIUM	Ir	192.2	THE TRIADS

From iris, or rainbow, so named for its colourful salts, discovered 1804. Very hard and hence extremely difficult to work or cast, iridium hardens other metals. Its alloys make bars used as standard weights and measures. The international 'standard metre' is platinum-iridium.

Atomic Number	*Element*	*Symbol*	*Atomic Weight*	*Family*
78	PLATINUM	Pt	195.08	THE TRIADS

From platina, or little silver; discovered 16th century. Found in nuggets of up to 21 pounds, it is used not only in weights and measures but also in catalysts, delicate instruments and electrical equipment. Its cost (more than gold) has demanded a hallmark for platinum jewellery.

79	GOLD	Au	196.97	LATE TRANS METALS

From the old English word geolo, or yellow; symbol Au from its Latin name aurum; prehistoric; the most malleable metal. Man's lust for gold has been a delusion, for he has pursued little more than a yellow gleam. It cannot be used for much besides money, jewellery and dental work.

80	MERCURY	Hg	200.59	LATE TRANS METALS

From the planet Mercury; symbol Hg from hydrargyrum, or liquid silver; prehistoric. It appears in the glass tubing of thermometers and barometers; it also finds use in 'silver' dental inlays and in silent electric switches. Vaporised mercury fills modern blue-hued street lights.

81	THALLIUM	Tl	204.38	BORON/CARBON

From thallos, or a young shoot – its spectrum is a bright-green line; discovered 1861. Its chief use is in thallium sulphate – a deadly rat poison. Odourless and tasteless, it is mixed with starch, sugar, glycerine and water to make an inviting if ominous 'treat' for household rodents.

82	LEAD	Pb	207.2	BORON/CARBON

From old English lead; symbol Pb from its Latin name, plumbum, also the origin of plumber. Prehistoric. Enormously durable, lead has been the backbone of plumbing for centuries. Lead pipes once used to drain the baths of ancient Rome have been uncovered still in working order.

83	BISMUTH	Bi	208.98	NITROGEN/OXYGEN

From the German wissmuth, or white mass; discovered 1450. The most metallic member of its family, bismuth melts at 271°C but forms alloys that melt at as low as 47°C. These find wide application in electric fuses, solders and in automatic fire-sprinkler systems.

84	POLONIUM	Po	(209)	NITROGEN/OXYGEN

After Poland; found in 1898 by Pierre and Marie Curie in pitchblende. The scarcest natural element, it was the first to be discovered by the Curies. It is sold as an alpha-particle source for scientific use.

Atomic Number	*Element*	*Symbol*	*Atomic Weight*	*Family*
85	ASTATINE	At	210	THE HALOGENS

From astatos, or unstable; discovered 1940. Astatine, prepared by bombarding bismuth atoms with helium nuclei, is radioactive and has a maximum half-life of 8.3 hours. Its detection is recorded in the notebook of one of its discoverers, American physicist D. R. Corson.

86	RADON	Rn	222	NOBLE GASES

From radium; discovered 1900. Heaviest gaseous element, it is emitted by radium and is itself radioactive; it decays into radioactive polonium and alpha rays. This radiation makes radon useful in cancer therapy; gold needles filled with the gas are implanted into the diseased tissue.

87	FRANCIUM	Fr	223	ALKALINE

From France; discovered 1939. A short-lived product of the decay of actinium, francium has never actually been seen. A graph identifies francium by its radiation in the notebook of its discoverer, Marguerite Perey, a one-time assistant to Marie Curie.

88	RADIUM	Ra	226	ALKALINE

From radius, or ray; discovered 1898 by Pierre and Marie Curie; sixth rarest of the elements. Radium bromide mixed with zinc sulphide is a mixture used in luminous watch dials. The radium gives off dangerous radiation which causes the zinc sulphide to glow.

89	ACTINIUM	Ac	227	ACTINIDE

From aktinos, or ray; discovered 1899. Second rarest of the elements. Found in pitchblende. With a half-life of 22 years, actinium decomposes into francium and helium.

90	THORIUM	Th	232.04	ACTINIDE

From Thor, Scandinavian war-god; discovered 1828. Thorium can be used instead of scarce uranium as a reactor fuel because it is readily converted into uranium. Almost as abundant as lead, earthly thorium stores more energy than all uranium, coal, oil and other fuels combined.

91	PROTACTINIUM	Pa	231	ACTINIDE

From protos, or first; it is the parent of actinium, which is formed by its radioactive decay; discovered 1917. Third rarest of the elements, it can be prepared by modern chemical techniques from thorium or uranium.

92	URANIUM	U	238.03	ACTINIDE

After the planet Uranus; discovered 1789; the heaviest atom among the natural elements. Its most common form has a half-life of 4,500 million years. In a nuclear reactor, it generates neutrons to keep the chain reaction going.

Atomic Number	*Element*	*Symbol*	*Atomic Weight*	*Family*
93	NEPTUNIUM	Np	237	ACTINIDE

After Neptune, the planet beyond Uranus; discovered 1940. Detected first in invisible, unweighable amounts, neptunium was the first 'synthetic' element made from uranium. Traces of it turn up in uranium ores, produced by stray neutrons from uranium's decay.

94	PLUTONIUM	Pu	244	ACTINIDE

After Pluto, the planet beyond Neptune; discovered 1940. Plutonium was used, instead of uranium in several of the first atomic bombs. In one of the codes of wartime physicists, plutonium was referred to as 'copper'; copper itself had to be renamed 'honest-to-God copper'.

95	AMERICIUM	Am	243	ACTINIDE

Named after the Americas, by analogy with the rare earth europium; discovered 1944. Americium is produced by bombarding plutonium with neutrons. It has been made in gramme quantities which, in the world of such elements, is virtually a superabundance.

96	CURIUM	Cm	247	ACTINIDE

In honour of Pierre and Marie Curie, pioneers in the field of radioactivity; discovered 1944. Curium, with a half-life of 19 years, is a decay product of americium. Curium hydroxide is the first known curium compound.

97	BERKELIUM	Bk	247	ACTINIDE

After Berkeley, the home of the University of California, whose scientists have detected all 11 of the transuranium elements; discovered 1949. Many inifinitesimal samples of berkelium have been prepared.

98	CALIFORNIUM	Cf	251	ACTINIDE

After the State and University of California; discovered 1950. Not until 1960 did californium exist in visible amounts.

99	EINSTEINIUM	Es	252	ACTINIDE

After Albert Einstein; discovered 1952. It was first detected in the debris from the 1952 H-bomb explosion at Eniwetok in the Pacific after tons of radioactive coral from atolls in the blast area were sifted and examined. The element was later made in a nuclear reactor.

100	FERMIUM	Fm	257	ACTINIDE

After Enrico Fermi; discovered 1953. Fermium, like einsteinium, was first isolated from the debris of the 1952 H-bomb test, having been produced from the fission of uranium. Because of its short life-span, scientists doubt that enough fermium will ever be obtained to be weighed.

Atomic Number	*Element*	*Symbol*	*Atomic Weight*	*Family*
101	MENDELEVIUM	Md	258	ACTINIDE

After Dmitri Mendeleyev, who devised the periodic table; discovered in 1955. Bombarding the scantest unweighable quantities of einsteinium with helium nuclei, scientists identified mendelevium from the barest shred of evidence – one to three atoms per bombardment.

102	NOBELIUM	No	259	ACTINIDE

After Alfred Nobel. A 1957 claim of discovery is disputed, but nobelium was positively identified in 1958 by a team of University of California scientists. Observations were not made on nobelium itself but on atoms of fermium 250 – 'daughter atoms' produced by nobelium's decay.

103	LAWRENCIUM	Lr	260	ACTINIDE

After Ernest O. Lawrence. Discovered in 1961 at Lawrence Radiation Laboratories, lawrencium was made by bombardment of californium with boron in a chamber fitted with a copper conveyor; the new atoms, one at a time, were carried to a radiation detector for identification.

104	UNNILQUADIUM	Unq	261	ACTINIDE

Originally named after Lord Ernest Rutherford, was produced in 1969 at Lawrence Radiation Laboratory by bombardment of californium with carbon nuclei. Soviet scientists had earlier announced the discovery of element 104, but this was not accepted internationally.

105	UNNIPENTIUM	Unp	262	ACTINIDE

Originally named after Otto Hahn of Germany, one of the discoverers of uranium fission. It was synthesized in 1970 by bombardment of californium with nitrogen nuclei. The name of this element was recently confirmed by the International Union of Pure and Applied Chemistry.

Once you have memorised the basic elements, and understood their properties, your brain is set for one of the most fascinating adventures imaginable!

CHAPTER FIFTEEN

THE RED WINES OF BORDEAUX

Memorise the following list, and you will have memorised one hundred of the greatest wines produced in the last few decades!

In so doing you will have laid the foundations for an on-going and on-growing knowledge of wines, will have made your dinner-time conversation more entrancing, will have increased the probability that you will listen to and remember new data concerning wines, will have enhanced your ability to discriminate and distinguish different wine tastes, will have added to your ability to use your synaesthetic memory, and will probably have increased the frequency with which you receive such wines as gifts!

Cheers!

Region	*Chateaux*	*Vintage*	*Growth*	*Mature*	*Rating*
St-Estephe Description: Blackcurrant fruit, massive	**Cos D'Estournel**	1982	2nd	1995–2020	97
St-Estephe Fruity, tannic, big	**Cos D'Estournel**	1961	2nd	1986–2000	91
Pauillac Fruity lushness, big	**Latour**	1982	1st	1995–2025	97
Pauillac Velvety, spicy oak	**Latour**	1981	1st	1991–2005	90
Pauillac Stunningly big bouquet, black-currant fruit	**Latour**	1978	1st	1992–2010	95
Pauillac Whiff of cedar and walnuts	**Latour**	1975	1st	2000–2030	93
Pauillac Very concentrated and dense	**Latour**	1970	1st	2000–2030	96

Region	*Chateaux*	*Vintage*	*Growth*	*Mature*	*Rating*
Pauillac Bouquet of leather, spices and tobacco	**Latour**	1966	1st	1988–2005	95
Pauillac Rich, round, supple	**Latour**	1964	1st	Now–1997	92
Pauillac Concentrated, rich flavours	**Latour**	1962	1st	1985–1995	91
Pauillac Syrupy, port-like, phenomenal bouquet	**Latour**	1961	1st	2000–2050	100
Pauillac Opulence, concentration	**Mouton-Rothschild**	1982	1st	1995–2025	100
Pauillac Dusty, leathery texture, chewy	**Mouton-Rothschild**	1975	1st	1995–2020	90
Pauillac Herbaceous aromas, powerful	**Mouton-Rothschild**	1970	1st	1995–2030	95
Pauillac Tightly restrained flavour, evolving bouquet	**Mouton-Rothschild**	1966	1st	1990–2010	92
Pauillac Olfactory, silky	**Mouton-Rothschild**	1962	1st	Now/ drink up!	90
Pauillac Fat on palate, multiscented bouquet	**Mouton-Rothschild**	1961	1st	1992–2020	96
Pauillac Tough, fleshy texture, impressive	**Lafite-Rothschild**	1983	1st	2005–2035	92
Pauillac Huge bouquet, concentrated	**Lafite-Rothschild**	1982	1st	2000–2030	96
Pauillac Promising, full bodied	**Lafite-Rothschild**	1981	1st	2000–2025	93

Region	*Chateaux*	*Vintage*	*Growth*	*Mature*	*Rating*
Pauillac Tight but complex bouquet, medium body	**Lafite-Rothschild**	1979	1st	1988–2005	90
Pauillac Ripe, savoury and fruity	**Lafite-Rothschild**	1978	1st	1988–2005	90
Pauillac Stunning, beautiful seductive bouquet	**Lafite-Rothschild**	1976	1st	1990–2010	96
Pauillac Cedary, fruity, explodes, full body	**Lafite-Rothschild**	1975	1st	1990–2010	96
Pauillac Intense bouquet, violet-scented fruit, full bodied	**Pichon-Longueville**	1983	2nd	1995–2015	94
Pauillac Intensely fruity, viscous wine	**Pichon-Longueville**	1982	2nd	1992–2010	94
Pauillac Supple, fat, silky	**Pichon-Longueville**	1981	2nd	1988–1998	91
Pauillac Velvety, rich and gentle	**Pichon-Longueville**	1979	2nd	1987–1998	93
Pauillac Deepest, richest and lush	**Pichon-Longueville**	1978	2nd	1988–2005	94
Pauillac Ripe, plummy fruit and fresh robustness	**Pichon-Longueville**	1975	2nd	1990–2010	92
Pauillac Big, rich, bouquet exotic	**Pichon-Longueville**	1970	2nd	1986–2000	91
Pauillac Dark, plummy bouquet, viscous	**Pichon-Longueville**	1961	2nd	Now–2003	95

Region	*Chateaux*	*Vintage*	*Growth*	*Mature*	*Rating*
St-Julien Voluptuous, stunning density	**Ducru-Beaucaillou**	1982	2nd	1994–2015	96
St-Julien Deft, touch of oak, ageing, beautifully crafted wine	**Ducru-Beaucaillou**	1981	2nd	1993–2008	90
St-Julien Deep, savoury flavours and multi-dimensional bouquet	**Ducru-Beaucaillou**	1978	2nd	1990–2015	90
St-Julien Ripe fruit and spicy oak, charm and appeal	**Ducru-Beaucaillou**	1970	2nd	1986–2000	91
St-Julien Exotic bouquet, rich, caressing the palate	**Ducru-Beaucaillou**	1961	2nd	Now–1992	93
St-Julien An infant giant, explosively fruity	**Leoville-Las Cases**	1983	2nd	1998–2020	90
St-Julien Monumental, intense and tannic	**Leoville-Las Cases**	1982	2nd	2000–2030	97
St-Julien Immense potential, full deep flavours, stunning	**Leoville-Las Cases**	1978	2nd	1994–2015	92
St-Julien Deep, ripe bouquet, aggressively tannic	**Leoville-Las Cases**	1975	2nd	1995–2030	92
St-Julien Perfectly balanced and excellent fruity intensity	**Leoville-Las Cases**	1966	2nd	1966–1997	90

Region	*Chateaux*	*Vintage*	*Growth*	*Mature*	*Rating*
St-Julien Plummy, extract of fruit	**Gruaud-Larose**	1983	2nd	1995–2015	90
St-Julien Incredibly rich, deliciously viscous, extremely tannic	**Gruaud-Larose**	1982	2nd	1995–2015	96
St-Julien Mouth puckering tannins, promising bouquet	**Gruaud-Larose**	1975	2nd	1995–2025	90
St-Julien Powerful, fresh, densely concentrated	**Gruaud-Larose**	1961	2nd	1987–2020	95
Margaux/ S. Medoc Astonishingly rich, concentrated, deep flavours	**Margaux**	1983	1st	1998–2030	96
Margaux/ S. Medoc Celestial wine, richly textured fruit and significant tannins	**Margaux**	1982	1st	1995–2025	96
Margaux/ S. Medoc Precocious and less weighty, concentrated tannic	**Margaux**	1981	1st	1991–2010	92
Margaux/ S. Medoc Tell-tale haunting, violet aroma	**Margaux**	1979	1st	1990–2005	93
Margaux/ S. Medoc Harmony and secuctive bouquet	**Margaux**	1978	1st	1990–2015	94

Region	*Chateaux*	*Vintage*	*Growth*	*Mature*	*Rating*
Margaux/ S. Medoc Top flight, intense bouquet	**Margaux**	1961	1st	1987–1992	92
Margaux/ S. Medoc Full intensity, plummy, chewy, powerful	**Palmer**	1983	3rd	1995–2010	90
Margaux/ S. Medoc Superstar, peppery, velvety	**Palmer**	1978	3rd	1989–2005	91
Margaux/ S. Medoc Uncommonly powerful, loaded with fruit and tannin	**Palmer**	1975	3rd	1990–2020	92
Margaux/ S. Medoc Intense, berryish aroma, full bodied	**Palmer**	1970	3rd	1988–2005	94
Margaux/ S. Medoc Sensational bouquet, velvety richness	**Palmer**	1966	3rd	1986–2000	96
Margaux/ S. Medoc Perfumed, opulent, multi-dimensional	**Palmer**	1961	3rd	1987–1992	96
Graves Monumental huge, spicy	**La Mission-Haut-Brion**	1982	Cru Classé	1994–2015	95
Graves Prominent vanillin, cassis fruit	**La Mission-Haut-Brion**	1981	Cru Classé	1991–2000	90
Graves Gravelly, scented bouquet, fruity flavours	**La Mission-Haut-Brion**	1978	Cru Classé	1990–2010	94

Region	*Chateaux*	*Vintage*	*Growth*	*Mature*	*Rating*
Graves Monumental magnificent iron-like mineral scents and smoky oak	**La Mission-Haut-Brion**	1975	Cru Classé	1990–2025	100
Graves Deep, spicy and full	**La Mission-Haut-Brion**	1970	Cru Classé	1990–2005	92
Graves Complex, cedary, tobacco-scented aroma	**La Mission-Haut-Brion**	1966	Cru Classé	1986–1995	91
Graves Enormous concentration of fruit, full intensity	**La Mission-Haut-Brion**	1964	Cru Classé	1987–1997	93
Graves Fabulous bouquet, full bodied	**La Mission-Haut-Brion**	1961	Cru Classé	1987–2010	96
Graves Gorgeous bouquet, vanillin oakiness, unctuous with layers of fruit	**Haut-Brion**	1982	1st	1995–2015	96
Graves Complex bouquet, earthy scents, balance, power, harmony	**Haut-Brion**	1979	1st	1992–2005	90
Graves Seductively rich, supple round and generous	**Haut-Brion**	1978	1st	1990–2000	90
Graves Splendidly rich, mineral scented, voluptuous flavours	**Haut-Brion**	1964	1st	1987–1995	90

Region	*Chateaux*	*Vintage*	*Growth*	*Mature*	*Rating*
Graves	**Haut-Brion**	1961	1st	1987–1992	93
Intensity of fruit, chewy texture, spicy bouquet					
Graves	**La Tour-Haut-Brion**	1982	Cru Classé	1996–2015	94
Massive, exceptional length, tannic					
Graves	**La Tour-Haut-Brion**	1975	Cru Classé	1995–2020	96
Bouquet of great tration, explodes, full bodied					pene-
Graves	**La Tour-Haut-Brion**	1961	Cru Classé	1990–2030	95
Chewy, opulent, massively proportioned					
Pomerol	**Petrus**	1982	Unclas.	1995–2030	100
Voluptuous, decadently concentrated fruit					
Pomerol	**Petrus**	1981	Unclas.	1997–2025	95
Bouquet explodes, grilled almonds and toffee, multi-dimensional					
Pomerol	**Petrus**	1979	Unclas.	1993–2015	92
Large framed, tannic, dense					
Pomerol	**Petrus**	1975	Unclas.	2000–2050	98
Blockbuster, opulent, massive					
Pomerol	**Petrus**	1971	Unclas.	1987–2000	95
Velvety, silky ripe fruit					
Pomerol	**Petrus**	1970	Unclas.	1990–2020	93
Jammy, full bodied					
Pomerol	**Petrus**	1967	Unclas.	1987–1994	90
Chunky, fleshy, warm and generous					

Region	*Chateaux*	*Vintage*	*Growth*	*Mature*	*Rating*
Pomerol Intense aromas, powerful, multi-dimensional	**Petrus**	1964	Unclas.	1987–1997	97
Pomerol Warm melted buttery caramel and toasty vanillin oak	**Petrus**	1961	Unclas.	1987–2003	100
Pomerol Avalanche of rich, ripe fruit, hint of fresh leather	**Trotanoy**	1982	Unclas.	1997–2020	96
Pomerol Fleshy, full body and bouquet	**Trotanoy**	1975	Unclas.	1988–2010	93
Pomerol Velvety, ripe, decadent, young	**Trotanoy**	1971	Unclas.	1985–1992	92
Pomerol Proportioned, broodingly dark	**Trotanoy**	1970	Unclas.	1990–2006	90
Pomerol Massively rich, unctuous texture, sweet	**Trotanoy**	1961	Unclas.	1987–2007	95
Pomerol Unbelievable bouquet, full bodied, viscous	**Lafleur**	1975	Unclas.	1990–2015	96
Pomerol Succulent, staggering concentration, sensational bouquet	**Latour a Pomerol**	1961	Unclas.	1987–1997	98
Pomerol Explosive, jammy, intense, voluptuous	**L'Evangile**	1982	Unclas.	1992–2005	96

Region	*Chateaux*	*Vintage*	*Growth*	*Mature*	*Rating*
St-Emilion Big-boned, deeply concentrated	**Cheval Blanc**	1983	Prem. Grand Cru Classé	1995–2020	93
St-Emilion Exotic aroma, intense fruit interplay, opulent	**Cheval Blanc**	1982	Prem. Grand Cru Classé	1992–2015	98
St-Emilion Relatively rich, plummy, silky, layered flavours	**Cheval Blanc**	1981	Prem. Grand Cru Classé	1989–2000	90
St-Emilion The best weight and richness, bouquet, full bodied	**Cheval Blanc**	1975	Prem. Grand Cru Classé	1990–2020	92
St-Emilion Powerful yet restrained, new wood and gravelly	**Cheval Blanc**	1964	Prem. Grand Cru Classé	1985–2000	95
St-Emilion Earthy, gravelly and full-blown bouquet	**Cheval Blanc**	1961	Prem. Grand Cru Classé	1987–?	94
St-Emilion Full bodied, jammy and rich	**Ausone**	1983	Prem. Grand Cru Classé	1992–2005	90
St-Emilion Concentrated, full bodied, backward	**Ausone**	1982	Prem. Grand Cru Classé	2000–2040	94
St-Emilion Voluptuous, intense, complex bouquet	**Ausone**	1976	Prem. Grand Cru Classé	1988–2000	90

CHAPTER SIXTEEN

THE SOLAR SYSTEM

During the last five centuries, mankind has discovered, with accelerating knowledge and fascination, that the neighbouring planets (wanderers) of our Solar System are not simply barren rocks. Each is an astonishingly different world, each with its own vast array of mysteries still to be solved, and each with its own part to play in our search for information about our own origins.

Our Solar System's Planets include one with a surface as hot as a furnace; one with a thick blanket of clouds that veils her secrets from us and through which we are just beginning to probe; one with a surface like the deserts of Australia, and which may well sustain life; one that is bigger than all the others put together, and which has a gigantic red eye which is still not fully explained, that would swallow the Earth; one with giant rings around it and strange moons which may harbour life; one covered by vast oceans of liquid gas and a core that resembles Earth; and two that are being explored as you read this book.

At this point in history, our Solar System is to us as the rest of the world was to the first European explorers; the great unknown, the arena for our next great explorations and adventures, and the environment which many of our children, grandchildren and great-grandchildren will call home.

Thus a knowledge of our Solar System will give you your first intellectual grappling hooks into a knowledge and understanding of the Universe. In so doing, it will give you a greater understanding and perspective of your place in the scheme of all things, and will make you a part of two of man's greatest intellectual voyages: the journeys to discover the secrets of the brain and the secrets of the Universe.

In this particular 'Memory Area', you are *already* an embryonic expert, for your have mastered the initial exercises and attendant explanation on pages 13 and 17.

This chapter encourages you to expand on this already expanding area of your knowledge, and to continue your journey . . .

THE SOLAR SYSTEM

	Mercury	*Venus*	*Earth*	*Mars*	*Jupiter*	*Saturn*	*Uranus*	*Neptune*	*Pluto*
Mean Distance from Sun (millions of miles)	36.0	67.1	92.9	141.5	483.4	886.7	1,782.7	2,794.3	3,666.1
Diameter (equatorial) (thousands of miles)	3,031	7,521	7,926	4,221	88,734	74,566	31,566	30,199	1,864
Mass (Earth=1)	0.055	0.814	1.000	0.107	317.8	95.16	14.55	17.23	0.0026(?)
Density (Water=1)	5.43	5.24	5.52	3.93	1.33	0.71	1.31	1.77	1.1
Volume (Earth=1)	0.06	0.86	1.00	0.15	1.323	752	64	54	0.01
Revolution around Sun	38.0 days	224.7 days	365.26 days	687.0 days	11.86 yrs	29.46 yrs	84.01 yrs	164.8 yrs	247.7 yrs
Rotation Period (days)	58.65	243.0	0.9973	1.0260	0.410	0.427	0.45	0.67	6.3867
Mean Orbital Speed (miles per second)	29.8	21.7	18.6	14.9	8.0	6.0	4.2	3.3	2.9
Inclination of Orbit (to Earth's Orbital Plane)	7.0	3.4	0.0	1.8	1.3	2.5	0.8	1.8	17.2
Gravity (Earth=1)	0.38	0.90	1.00	0.38	2.53	1.07	0.92	1.19	0.05(?)
Moons	–	–	Moon	Phobos Deimos	Metis Adrastea Amalthea Thebe Io Europa Ganymede Callisto Leda Himalia Lysithea Elara Ananke Carme Pasiphae Sinope	Atlas 1980S27 1980S26 Janus Epimetheus Mimas Enceladus Tethys Telesto Calypso Dione 1980S6 Rhea Titan Hyperion Iapetus Phoebe	Miranda Ariel Umbriel Titania Oberon	Triton Nereid	Charon

The asteroids are huge chunks of rock, orbiting the sun between Mars and Jupiter. They are minor planets. There may be as many as 40,000 of them.

CHAPTER SEVENTEEN

MEMORISING YOUR LIFE

If you wish to remember the major elements of your past, present and future life, SEM^3 enables you to do so with ease.

Allow one key memory word for each month. In so doing, it is possible for you, by adding a few major items for the month on a Link System, to remember eight years within 100 key image words in the Self-Enhancing Master Memory Matrix.

The memorisation of your life can be made much more easy and enjoyable by using a diary/self-management system such as the Universal Personal Organiser (UPO). Such a system makes use of all the Memory Foundations and Principles, organises the year, months and days in such a way as to enable you to use all your cortical and memory skills, and allows you to record, using Mind Maps and the Memory Principles, all those important aspects of your life that you consider memorable.

The dream of memorising an entire life has been one of the 'mental holy grails' of the human race. It is now easily within your grasp.

The following chapter tells of such a dream come true.

CHAPTER EIGHTEEN

MEMORISING A LIFE: THE STORY OF FUNES THE MEMORIOUS

The following story by Jorge Luis Borges exemplifies what was discussed in the previous chapter. Critics are still trying to determine whether the story was a fabrication, a brilliant work of imagination, or a true reportage.

In view of what you have read so far, decide for yourself: is it possible? did Funes really exist? is the story true?!

FUNES, THE MEMORIOUS

'I remember him (I scarcely have the right to use this ghostly verb; only one man on earth deserved the right, and he is dead), I remember him with a dark passionflower in his hand, looking at it as no one has ever looked at such a flower, though they might look from the twilight of day until the twilight of night, for a whole life long. I remember him, his face immobile and Indian-like, and singularly *remote*, behind his cigarette. I remember (I believe) the strong delicate fingers of the plainsman who can braid leather. I remember, near those hands, a vessel in which to make maté tea, bearing the arms of the Banda Oriental;* I remember, in the window of the house, a yellow rush mat, and beyond, a vague marshy landscape. I remember clearly his voice, the deliberate, resentful nasal voice of the old Eastern Shore man, without the Italianate syllables of today, I did not see him more than three times; the last time, in 1887 . . .

That all those who knew him should write something about him seems to me a very felicitous idea; my testimony may perhaps be the briefest and without doubt the poorest, and it will not be the least impartial. The deplorable fact of my being an Argentinian will hinder me from falling into a dithyramb

*The Eastern Shore (of the Uruguay River); now the Orient Republic of Uruguay. – *Editor's note.*

– an obligatory form in the Uruguay, when the theme is an Uruguayan.

Littérateur, slicker, Buenos Airean: Funes did not use these insulting phrases, but I am sufficiently aware that for him I represented these unfortunate categories. Pedro Leandro Ipuche has written that Funes was a precursor of the superman, "an untamed and vernacular Zarathustra"; I do not doubt it, but one must not forget, either, that he was a countryman from the town of Fray Bentos, with certain incurable limitations.

My first recollection of Funes is quite clear, I see him at dusk, sometimes in March or February of the year '84. That year, my father had taken me to spend the summer at Fray Bentos. I was on my way back from the farm at San Francisco with my cousin Bernardo Haedo. We came back singing, on horseback; and this last fact was not the only reason for my joy. After a sultry day, an enormous slate-grey storm had obscured the sky. It was driven on by a wind from the south; the trees were already tossing like madmen; and I had the apprehension (the secret hope) that the elemental downpour would catch us out in the open. We were running a kind of race with the tempest. We rode into a narrow lane which wound down between two enormously high brick footpaths. It had grown black of a sudden; I now heard rapid almost secret steps above; I raised my eyes and saw a boy running along the narrow, cracked path as if he were running along a narrow, broken wall. I remember the loose trousers, tight at the bottom, the hemp sandals; I remember the cigarette in the hard visage, standing out against the by now limitless darkness. Bernardo unexpectedly yelled to him: "What's the time, Ireneo?" Without looking up, without stopping, Ireneo replied: "In ten minutes it will be eight o'clock, child Bernardo Juan Francisco". The voice was sharp, mocking.

I am so absentminded that the dialogue which I have just cited would not have penetrated my attention if it had not been repeated by my cousin, who was stimulated, I think, by a certain local pride and by a desire to show himself indifferent to the other's three-sided reply.

He told me that the boy above us in the pass was a certain Ireneo Funes, renowned for a number of eccentricities, such as that of having nothing to do with people and of always knowing the time, like a watch. He added that Ireneo was the son of María Clementine Funes, an ironing woman in the town, and that his father, some people said, was an "Englishman" named O'Connor, a doctor in the salting fields, though some said the father was a horse-breaker, or scout, from the province of El Salto. Ireneo lived with his mother, at the edge of the country house of the Laurels.

In the years '85 and '86 we spent the summer in the city of Montevideo. We returned to Fray Bentos in '87. As was natural, I inquired after all my acquaintances, and finally, about "the chronometer Funes". I was told that he had been thrown by a wild horse at the San Francisco ranch, and that he had been hopelessly crippled. I remember the impression of uneasy magic which the news provoked in me: the only time I had seen him we were on horseback, coming from San Francisco, and he was in a high place; from the lips of my cousin Bernardo the affair sounded like a dream elaborated with elements out of the past. They told me that Ireneo did not move now from his cot, but remained with his eyes fixed on the backyard fig tree, or on a cobweb. At sunset he allowed himself to be brought to the window. He carried pride to the extreme of pretending that the blow which had befallen him was a good thing . . . Twice I saw him behind the iron gate which sternly delineated his eternal imprisonment: unmoving, once, his eyes closed; unmoving also, another time, absorbed in the contemplation of a sweet-smelling sprig of lavender cotton.

At the time I had begun, not without some ostentation, the methodical study of Latin. My valise contained the *De viris illustribus* of Lhomond, the *Thesaurus* of Quicherat, *Caesar's Commentaries*, and an odd-numbered volume of the *Historia Naturalis* of Pliny, which exceeded (and still exceeds) my modest talents as a Latinist. Everything is noised around in a small town; Ireneo, at his small farm on the outskirts, was not long in learning of the arrival of these anomalous books. He sent me a flowery, ceremonious letter, in which he recalled our encounter, unfortunately brief, "on the seventh day of February of the year '84," and alluded to the glorious services which Don Gregorio Haedo, my uncle, dead the same year, "had rendered to the Two Fatherlands in the glorious campaign of Ituzaingó," and he solicited the loan of any one of the volumes, to be accompanied by a dictionary "for the better intelligence of the original text, for I do not know Latin as yet." He promised to return them in good condition, almost immediately. The letter was perfect, very nicely constructed; the orthography was of the type sponsored by Andrés Bello: *i* for *y*, *j* for *g*. At first I naturally suspected a jest. My cousins assured me it was not so, that these were the ways of Ireneo. I did not know whether to attribute to impudence, ignorance, or stupidity, the idea that the difficult Latin required no other instrument than a dictionary; in order fully to undeceive him I sent the *Gradus ad Parnassum* of Quicherat, and the Pliny.

On 14 February, I received a telegram from Buenos Aires telling me to return immediately, for my father was "in no way well." God forgive me, but the prestige of being the recipient of an urgent telegram, the desire to point out to all of Fray Bentos the contradiction between the negative form of the news and the positive adverb, the temptation to dramatize my sorrow as I feigned a virile stoicism, all no doubt distracted me from the possibility of anguish. As I packed my valise, I noticed that I was missing the *Gradus* and the volume of the *Historia Naturalis*. The *Saturn* was to weigh anchor on the morning of the next day; that night, after supper, I made my way to the house of Funes. Outside, I was surprised to find the night no less oppressive than the day.

Ireneo's mother received me at the modest ranch.

She told me that Ireneo was in the back room and that I should not be disturbed to find him in the dark, for he knew how to pass the dead hours without lighting the candle. I crossed the cobblestone patio, the small corridor; I came to the second patio. A great vine covered everything, so that the darkness seemed complete. Of a sudden I heard the high-pitched, mocking voice of Ireneo. The voice spoke in Latin; the voice (which came out of the obscurity) was reading, with obvious delight, a treatise or prayer or incantation. The Roman syllables resounded in the earthen patio; my suspicion made them seem undecipherable, interminable; afterwards, in the enormous dialogue of that night, I learned that they made up the first paragraph of the twenty-fourth chapter of the seventh book of the *Historia Naturalis*. The subject of this chapter is memory; the last words are *ut nihil non iisdem verbis redderetur auditum.*

Without the least change in his voice, Ireneo bade me come in. He was lying on the cot, smoking. It seems to me that I did not see his face until dawn; I seem to recall the momentary glow of the cigarette. The room smelled vaguely of dampness. I sat down, and repeated the story of the telegram and my father's illness.

I come now to the most difficult point in my narrative. For the entire story has no other point (the reader might as well know it by now) than this dialogue of almost a half-century ago. I shall not attempt to reproduce his words, now irrecoverable. I prefer truthfully to make a résumé of the many things Ireneo told me. The indirect style is remote and weak; I know that I sacrifice the effectiveness of my narrative; but let my readers imagine the nebulous sentences which clouded that night.

Ireneo began by enumerating, in Latin and Spanish, the cases of prodigious memory cited in the *Historia Naturalis*: Cyrus, king of the Persians, who could call every soldier in his armies by name; Mithridates Eupator, who administered justice in the twenty-two languages of his empire; Simonides, inventor of mnemotechny; Metrodorus, who practised the art of repeating faithfully what he heard once. With evident good faith Funes marvelled that such things should be considered marvellous. He told me that previous to the rainy afternoon when the blue-tinted horse threw him, he had been – like any Christian – blind, deaf-mute, somnambulistic, memoryless. (I tried to remind him of his precise perception of time, his memory for proper names; he paid no attention to me.) For nineteen years, he said, he had lived like a person in a dream: he looked without seeing, heard without hearing, forgot everything – almost everything. On falling from the horse, he lost consciousness; when he recovered it, the present was almost intolerable it was so rich and bright; the same was true of the most ancient and most trivial memories. A little later he realized that he was crippled. This fact scarcely interested him. He reasoned (or felt) that immobility was a minimum price to pay. And now, his perception and his memory were infallible.

We, in a glance, perceive three wine glasses on the table; Funes saw all the shoots, clusters, and grapes of the vine. He remembered the shapes of the clouds in the south at dawn on the 30th of April of 1882, and he could compare them in his recollection with the marbled grain in the design of a leather-bound book which he had seen only once, and with the lines in the spray which an oar raised in the Rio Negro on the eve of the battle of the Quebracho. These recollections were not simple; each visual image was linked to muscular sensations, thermal sensations, etc. He could reconstruct all his dreams all his fancies. Two or three times he had reconstructed an entire day. He told me: *I have more memories in myself alone than all men have had since the world was a world.* And again: *My dreams are like your vigils.* And again, toward dawn: *My memory, sir, is like a garbage disposal.*

A circumference on a blackboard, a rectangular triangle, a rhomb, are forms which we can fully intuit; the same held true with Ireneo for the tempestuous mane of a stallion, a herd of cattle in a pass, the ever-changing flame or the innumerable ash, the many faces of a dead man during the course of a protracted wake. He could perceive I do not know how many stars in the sky.

These things he told me; neither then nor at any time later did they seem doubtful. In those days neither the cinema nor the phonograph yet existed; nevertheless, it seems strange, almost incredible, that no one should have experimented on Funes. The truth is that we all live by leaving behind; no doubt we all profoundly know that we are immortal and that sooner or later every man will do all things and know everything.

The voice of Funes, out of the darkness, continued. He told me that toward 1886 he had devised a new system of enumeration and that in a very few days he had gone beyond twenty-four thousand. He had not written it down, for what he once mediated would not be erased. The first stimulus to his work, I believe, had been his discontent with the fact that "thirty-three Uruguayans" required two symbols and three words, rather than a single word and a single symbol. Later he applied his extravagant principle to the other numbers. In place of seven thousand thirteen, he would say (for example)

Máximo Perez; in place of seven thousand fourteen, *The Train*; other numbers were *Luis Melián Lafinur, Olimar, Brimstone, Clubs, The Whale, Gas, The Cauldron, Napoleon, Agustín de Vedia*. In lieu of five hundred, he would say *nine*. Each word had a particular sign, a species of mark; the last were very complicated . . . I attempted to explain that this rhapsody of unconnected terms was precisely the contrary of a system of enumeration. I said that to say three hundred and sixty-five was to say three hundreds, six tens, five units: an analysis which does not exist in such numbers as *The Negro Timoteo* or *The Flesh Blanket*. Funes did not understand me, or did not wish to understand me.

Locke, in the seventeenth century, postulated (and rejected) an impossible idiom in which each individual object, each stone, each bird and branch had an individual name; Funes had once projected an analogous idiom, but he had renounced it as being too general, too ambiguous. In effect, Funes not only remembered every leaf on every tree of every wood, but even every one of the times he had preceived or imagined it. He determined to reduce all of his past experience to some seventy thousand recollections, which he would later define numerically. Two considerations dissuaded him: the thought that the task was interminable and the thought that it was useless. He knew that at the hour of his death he would scarcely have finished classifying even all the memories of his childhood.

The two projects I have indicated (an infinite vocabulary for the natural series of numbers, and a usable mental catalogue of all the images of memory) are lacking in sense, but they reveal a certain stammering greatness. They allow us to make out dimly, or to infer, the dizzying world of Funes. He was, let us not forget, almost incapable of general, platonic ideas. It was not only difficult for him to understand that the generic term *dog* embraced so many unlike specimens of differing sizes and different forms; he was disturbed by the fact that a dog at three-fourteen (seen in profile) should have the same name as the dog at three-fifteen (seen from the front). His own face in the mirror, his own hands, surprised him on every occasion. Swift writes that the emperor of Lilliput could discern the movement of the minute hand; Funes could continuously make out the tranquil advances of corruption, of caries, of fatigue. He noted the progress of death, of moisture. He was the solitary and lucid spectator of a multiform world which was instantaneously and almost intolerably exact. Babylon, London, and New York have overawed the imagination of men with their ferocious splendour; no one, in those populous towers or upon those surging avenues, has felt the heat and pressure of a reality as indefatigable as that which day and night converged upon the unfortunate Ireneo in his humble South American farmhouse. It was very difficult for him to sleep. To sleep is to be abstracted from the world; Funes, on his back in his cot, in the shadows, imagined every crevice and every moulding of the various houses which surrounded him. (I repeat, the least important of his recollections was more minutely precise and more lively than our perception of a physical pleasure or a physical torment.) Toward the east, in a section which was not yet cut into blocks of homes, there were some new unknown houses. Funes imagined them black, compact, made of a single obscurity; he would turn his face in this direction in order to sleep. He would also imagine himself at the bottom of the river, being rocked and annihilated by the current.

Without effort, he had learned English, French, Portuguese, Latin. I suspect, nevertheless, that he was not very capable of thought. To think is to forget a difference, to generalize, to abstract. In the overly replete world of Funes there was nothing but details, almost contiguous details.

The equivocal clarity of dawn penetrated along the earthen patio.

Then it was that I saw the face of the voice which had spoken all through the night. Ireneo was nineteen years old; he had been born in 1868; he seemed as monumental as bronze, more ancient than Egypt, anterior to the prophecies and the pyramids. It occurred to me that each one of my words (each one of my gestures) would live on in his implacable memory; I was benumbed by the fear of multiplying superfluous gestures.

Ireneo Funes died in 1889, of a pulmonary congestion.'

1942 *Translated by* ANTHONY KERRIGAN

(Taken from *Fictions* by *Jorge Luis Borges*, published by George Weidenfeld & Nicolson Limited)

CHAPTER NINETEEN

CONCLUSION AND YOUR FUTURE

Now that you have completed your first reading of *Master Your Memory*, you are well on the way to providing the essential 'software' for the incredible 'hardware' of your super-biocomputer brain.

This is a task that will give you greater mental power and greater joy for the remainder of your life.

Since the invention of SEM^3, an increasing number of people have become involved in networks and clubs designed to provide companions and help on this Fantastic Voyage.

On the following pages is information to help you if you are so inclined. . .

It has been a delight sharing memory with you; I similarly look forward to sharing *future* memories!

We are conducting a survey on Ireneo Funes, and will be delighted to hear whether you thought the story in Chapter Eighteen was true or false.

If you are interested in joining in the investigation, please send a note to the publisher with your opinion. The results will be published in the next edition.

APPENDIX

Tony Buzan

Tony Buzan is the originator of Mind Maps, the SEM^3 (Self-Enhancing Master Memory Matrix), the Group/Family/Work/Mind Map Study Technique, and new concepts in brain functioning relating to the process of Change and Metapositive Thinking. He is also the Founder of the International Brain Clubs and Buzan Centres.

Tony Buzan was born in London in 1942, emigrated to Vancouver in 1954 and graduated from the University of British Columbia in 1964, achieving double Honours in Psychology, English, Mathematics and the General Sciences. Returning to England in 1966, he worked on Fleet Street, also editing the International Journal of MENSA (the high IQ society).

Since then he has published ten books (nine on the brain and learning and one volume of poetry). His books have now been published in fifty countries and translated into twenty languages. *Use Your Head* has surpassed worldwide sales of a million, and is a standard introductory text for the Open University.

Tony Buzan has featured in, presented and co-produced many television, video and radio programmes, both national and international, including the record-breaking *Use Your Head* series (BBC TV); the *Open Mind* series (ITV); *The Enchanted Loom*, a one-hour feature documentary on the brain; and numerous talk shows. His latest video series, *Buzan Business Training*, is a three-part training package introducing the major elements of his work to the international business community.

He is advisor to royalty, governments, multi-national organisations, including IBM, BP, Barclays International, Digital Equipment Corporation, Buzan Mast, Management Centre Europe, General Motors, Bell Telephone, AT&T, Rank Xerox, and Nabisco, and is a regular lecturer at the leading international universities and schools.

He is a Fellow of the Institute of Training and Development, the Jamaican Institute of Management and the Swedish Management Group, and is an elected member of the International Faculty of the Young Presidents' Organisation and the International Council of Psychologists. A Member of the Institute of Directors, and a Freeman of the City of London, he is also advisor to the British Olympic Rowing Squad.

Products

Audio tapes

Learning and Memory – produced for *Psychology Today* magazine
The Intelligence Revolution (set of 3 tapes)
Tony Buzan on Memory and Advanced Mind Mapping.
Make the Most of Your Mind – based on the book of the same name, and *Harnessing the ParaBrain.*
Supercreativity and Mind Mapping – a comprehensive introduction to the workings of your brain, and the theory and use of Mind Mapping (with manuallette).

Video tapes

Use Your Head – the original nine part BBC TV series attractively presented with updated facilitator's manual and *Use Your Head* and *Use Your Memory* books.
The Enchanted Loom – documentary on the brain featuring interviews with the world's major contributors to the field devised and presented by Tony Buzan.
Buzan Business Training – complete business training course emphasising the application of Mind Mapping, Memory and Information Management to business.
Family Genius Training – complete video series based on *Use Your Head* and *Make the Most of Your Mind*, which guides the family through the latest information on brain and brain training.

Poster

'Body and Soul' Master Mind Map poster
A limited edition poster depicting, in a surrealist manner, all the principles taught by Tony Buzan. This beautiful picture is called 'Body and Soul' and each numbered copy is signed by the Swedish artist, Ulf Ekberg.

Mind Map Kits

Specially designed A3 and A4 pads and pens

Master Your Memory Matrix 0–10,000

Laminated 0–99 and 100 to 10,000 Matrix plus full instructions to assist the *Master Your Memory* reader. To order, contact

The Buzan Centre
Suite 2, Cardigan House,
37 Waterloo Road
Winton
Dorset BH9 1BD

Telephone enquiries to: 0202 533593
Fax: 0202 534572

The Brain Club

The Brain Club is an international organisation designed to help you increase your mental, physical and spiritual awareness. This is done by waking that sleeping giant, your brain, and teaching you how to access its vast intelligences, first by learning how to learn and then by developing specific skills in areas that you choose.

You can do this by studying in your own home, or meeting regularly with others who also wish to expand their vast range of mental skills as outlined in *Master Your Memory*.

Join these 'mental gymnasiums' and improve your following skill areas:

a. Memorising
b. Range/Speed Reading
c. Mind Mapping and Creative Thinking
d. Learning and Studying
e. I.Q.
f. Mathematics
g. The Arts
h. Physical Performance
i. Vocabulary Building/Language Learning
j. Communicating
k. Personality Development
l. Games Skills
m. Special Skills

Each area within The Brain Club will be graded and certificates awarded as you reach advancing levels of competence.

For details of the nearest cell of the Brain Club, contact

The Buzan Centre
Suite 2, Cardigan House,
37 Waterloo Road
Winton
Dorset BH9 1BD

Telephone enquiries to: 0202 533593
Fax: 0202 534572

The Universal Personal Organiser (UPO)

This **new** and **unique** approach to time and self-management is a diary system, based on the techniques created and taught by Tony Buzan.

The Universal Personal Organiser is a living system that **grows** with you, and that provides a comprehensive perspective on your life, your desires, and your business and family functions.

The Universal Personal Organiser is the first diary system to use the principles that Leonardo da Vinci discovered in the Italian Renaissance: that images and colour enhance both **creativity** and **memory**, as well as being more **enjoyable** and **easier** than regular diary systems.

The Universal Personal Organiser **reflects you**, and gives you the **freedom** to perform at your Highest Potential. The Universal Personal Organiser is made of materials that are of the **highest quality**, using the best leathers and paper available.

The Universal Personal Organiser is designed to help you manage the four main areas of life: **health** (mental, physical and emotional); **happiness (family), creativity and wealth.**

The Universal Personal Organiser, in so doing, allows you to **organise** your past, present and future in a manner that is both **enjoyable** and **fun.**

The Universal Personal Organiser's pages and partitions have been designed to enable you to get a comprehensive perspective on your **yearly plan**, your **monthly** and **weekly plans**, and your **daily plan**, using the new **twenty-four hour clock, mind mapping**, and *Master Your Memory* systems.

For further information on:

* Training courses based on Tony Buzan's methods
* Co-ordination of the Brain Club
* Supportive books, tapes and educational products

Contact

The Buzan Centre
Suite 2, Cardigan House
37 Waterloo Road
Winton
Dorset BH9 1BD

Telephone enquiries to: 0202 533593
Fax: 0202 534572

* Please send a stamped, self-addressed envelope for your reply.

Buzan Training Courses

Courses are prepared for:

* ⋆ Governments
* ⋆ Corporations
* ⋆ Schools and universities
* ⋆ Private groups and organisations
* ⋆ Foundations
* ⋆ Children
* ⋆ Families
* ⋆ Senior citizens

The courses are based on the following books by Tony Buzan:

* ⋆ Make the Most of Your Mind
* ⋆ Master Your Memory
* ⋆ Speed (and Range) Reading
* ⋆ Use Your Head
* ⋆ Use Your Memory
* ⋆ The Brain User's Guide
* ⋆ Harnessing the ParaBrain
* ⋆ Universal Personal Organiser

The courses emphasise:

* ⋆ Mind mapping
* ⋆ Memory skills – advanced
* ⋆ Speed reading – advanced
* ⋆ Learning to learn
* ⋆ Creativity
* ⋆ Presentation skills
* ⋆ Work/study skills
* ⋆ Corporate and family brain training
* ⋆ The ageing brain
* ⋆ Managing change
* ⋆ Personal and time management
* ⋆ Especially tailored courses

For enquiries, contact

The Buzan Centre
Suite 2, Cardigan House
37 Waterloo Road
Winton
Dorset BH9 1BD

Telephone enquiries to: 0202 533593
Fax: 0202 534572

INDEX